Awaken Your Sensual Goddess

Make Your Dreams Blossom

Dr. Rebecca Rosenblat

Clinical Sexologist, Psychotherapist, Media Personality

Manor House

Library and Archives Canada
Cataloguing in Publication

Title: Awaken your sensual goddess : make your dreams blossom / Dr. Rebecca Rosenblat, clinical sexologist, psychotherapist, media personality.

Names: Rosenblat, Rebecca, author.

Identifiers: Canadiana 20220424578 | ISBN 9781988058832 (hardcover) | ISBN 9781988058825 (softcover)

Subjects: LCSH: Women—Sexual behavior. | LCSH: Sensuality. | LCSH: Sexual excitement.

Classification: LCC HQ29 .R67 2022 | DDC 306.7082—dc23

Illustrations By: Marta McKenzie & Bojan Zoric

Cover art: olgaman / Shutterstock / (cherries in female mouth)

First Edition

Cover Design-layout / Interior- layout: Michael Davie
230 pages / Approx. 60,000 words. All rights reserved.
Published October 2022 / Copyright 2022
Manor House Publishing Inc.
452 Cottingham Crescent, Ancaster, ON, L9G 3V6
www.manor-house-publishing.com (905) 648-4797

This project has been made possible [in part] by the Government of Canada. « *Ce projet a été rendu possible [en partie] grâce au gouvernement du Canada.*

Funded by the Government of Canada
Financé par le gouvernement du Canada | Canada

To Carol Clark, for dedicating her life to healthy sexuality and for being an inspiration to me. And to Sonja Bruns, for teaching me to love myself just as I am, even while walking alongside me through my darkest hours.

Praise for *Awaken Your Sensual Goddess*:

"In a world where the vagina is stigmatized, shamed and where women are never encouraged to talk about... or indulge their pussies, this book is a revelation! Dr. Rosenblat has masterfully crafted this spectacular guide for every woman to help awaken her inner goddess and connect to the most powerful source of her being; the source of all human life and the bridge to her divine power. This book made me realize female power is pussy power and it's time women stop ignoring our lady parts and start embracing... our inner goddess!"
-**Jennifer Lieberman**, Best Selling author, *Year of the What?*

"This book is an uplifting celebration for all of us! For too long, women have gotten the message their bodies and sexuality are shameful, degrading, and even evil. Dr. Rosenblat turns that message on its head and promotes female power in the most positive terms. Women need to read this to take ownership of their divine selves and men need to read it to fully appreciate the gift of having confident and radiant women in the world!"
- **Dr. Carol Clark,** Director of the International Institute of Clinical Sexology and author of *My Pocket Therapist*

"In the Victorian Era, Freud dismissed female psychology as a yearning to be male. In the 21st Century, Dr. Rosenblat reveals the abundance of femininity in its own right. To be a Goddess is not to be a companion for gods. It is a power unto itself."
- **Amy Waterman**, author of *Unleash Your Pleasure Power*

"Dr. Rebecca Rosenblat is an insightful, highly trained and engaging communicator of all things sensual. Welcome her wisdom into your world...you won't regret it!"
- **Dr. Janis Roszler**, Clincal Sexologist, co-author, ***Sweet Romance - A Woman's Guide to Love and Intimacy with Diabetes***

"Rebecca brings to life the essence of feminine sensuality in this book. She shows how sexual empowerment is key to an intimate connection in relationships."
- **Barb Kirkham**, Psychotherapist, Sex Educator

Foreword

Society expects women to be caring, beautiful, and sensual. But when they invest in feeling good about themselves, indulging their sensuality, and fulfilling their own hopes and dreams, they're often discouraged. So they can become disconnected from their inner core, lose their *joie de vie*, and start to question their self-worth and life-purpose.

Awaken Your Sensual Goddess is geared towards awakening your inner goddess, so you can embrace your authentic self, feel empowered, fulfil your needs and desires, and connect with the sensuality that's in your design. And then, if you chose to invite a lover into your life, have the tools and the skillset to bring your A game, to attract and seduce in the most mind-blowing ways.

Clinical Sexologist and Media Personality, Dr. Rebecca Rosenblat-Billings will show you how to connect with the goddess mindset, love and accept yourself just as you are, and get rid of the mental static that holds you back. You'll be transformed into the woman who knows her self-worth, who'll never again put up with an unhealthy relationship, and who can bring her sexy on, to become the most enchanting lover, and live the life of her dreams, on her own terms!

It's the only book you'll ever need, for learning to accept and love yourself. And if you want a partner, the only book that will offer you step-by-step instruction in everything from meeting someone, to hooking them in, to keeping them.

Wipe the slate clean, set aside your inhibitions, give yourself the permission to become the delicious creature that you were meant to be, and pursue the opportunities that make your life exiting and fulfilling. It's time to invest in yourself, right now. Your exciting new life is waiting for you!

5

Table of Contents

PART A

CONNECTING WITH MY SENSUAL SELF

Introduction

When you hear the expression goddess, what image does your mind conjure up? Is she strong, sexy, exciting, fun, funny, living the life she craves? Is she a smart, brave, courageous, fierce femme, who's in charge of her life? Is she a trailblazer, a leader, creating the life she wants to be remembered for in her obituary? Is she fulfilling the hopes and dreams she had as a little girl, before she was discouraged and bound by the limitations placed on her?

Whoever she is, however you see her, she lives inside of you, waiting to be unleashed. And the fact that you're holding this book in your hands, means that you're ready for her to manifest herself – i.e., *You're* ready to manifest *Yourself.*

Coming into our own is the best thing we can do for ourselves. So I'm beyond excited that you've decided to invest in yourself and go on this journey; and I'm truly honoured to be your tour guide. You're in the right place, at the right time, right now!

In a culture where older women don't pass along their knowledge onto younger women, and teach them to love themselves, engage their sensuality, and intentionally connect with the spiritual and the sensual in others, I felt it was imperative that I write this book, for women of *all* ages, since we can *all* use some guidance. It's a woman to woman compendium with everything that you'll need to awaken your inner goddess, and live your life sensually, decadently and unapologetically.

So why should you listen to me anyway?

It's not because of the letters after my name, or years of research, education, and experience; it's because thousands of women have shared with me what they're feeling and missing, and at least as many men have shared what they hope for in their relationships, but rarely receive. There's little instruction to nurture what's in our nature – we're taught about so many things expect for living authentically in our zone, or nurturing our relationships to get the most out of them, both of which can make us sublimely happy.

We must embrace our needs and desires, and delight in enjoying our femaleness. It's in our design to live fulfilled lives, as powerful creatures and sensual lovers – if that's what our heart craves. The two can definitely go hand in hand; we just have to pay attention to our entire pallet of yearnings.

All I ask of you is, forget about what you've been told, wipe the slate clean, and allow me to help you listen to your heart, connect with your sensual inner goddess, and take advantage of centuries of hidden wisdom, found within a vast body of worldwide literature. It's time to celebrate being a woman, and take it to a magnificent art-form.

But since this is *your* personal journey, based in *your* desires, before you begin, you need to think about what makes *you* the happiest and what makes *you* the most miserable, independent of what you've been taught to think and feel. And what's stood in the way of you being the ideal and most sensual version of yourself? It's the only way you'll be able to create a life that's designed *by* you, *for* you.

Now close your eyes and imagine what your life would look like if you were to become that person, embodying the virtues mentioned above, and then some, because how you see your life is how you're going to live it.

Moving forward, you have to commit to living and acting that way – like dressing for the job you want versus the job you're in – until it becomes a reality. It'll help transform you in a way that's akin to what happens to a child when they don a Halloween costume – all fears and insecurities get replaced by power, confidence, and playfulness, as they slip into their desired character!

When my kids were little, we had a trunk full of kick-ass outfits, from dinosaurs and dragons to their favourite superheroes, to enrich their imaginations and create an unstoppable mindset, without limitations. And that trunk didn't just open up for Halloween – it was there for them to play "make belief" any time they wanted, so they'd never stop dreaming. Today, barely in their thirties, they're already highly accomplished, making their mark on the world, fuelled with the confidence that they can do anything they set their minds to, which ultimately gives them the drive to accomplish their goals.

It always starts with a dream, and a belief that we *can* make it happen if we want it badly enough. Once we make that decision, our inner goddess will rise to the occasion, and refuse to let us go to a place of self-doubt.

It is my sincerest hope that you'll invest in yourself the way you do in others, especially the person who depletes you the most, with their lack of reciprocity.

FYI, I also have every intention of awakening the *sex* goddess within you, since she's the mother of sensuality. She's driven by the strongest, most delicious, primal instincts – I'm getting a lady wood just thinking about her. And once *you* experience her yourself, you won't give a rat's ass about all the things that make you blush or second-guess yourself – I definitely don't, as you're about to find out.

Final word: even though I might use bio-gender, heteronormative terms, to make my delivery less complicated, I revel in the complicated in every other way. I fully celebrate all parts of you, regardless of your bio-gender, orientation, and the lifestyle you identify with; because that's the whole point of loving ourselves completely, in all our delightful incarnations, living life on our own terms!

1: Understanding the Goddess Mindset

A goddess embodies power, sensuality, deliberation, and she moves through life gracefully and unapologetically, because she isn't afraid of being authentic. She never questions herself, never puts herself down, and never compares herself to other goddesses, because she's focused on having fun and living life to the fullest, while helping other goddesses do the same – anything else is counterproductive.

To her, the more pleasure she gives, the more she receives, the more it multiplies. So she's committed to studying pleasure and desire to the last infinitesimal detail, to develop her craft, and become equally apt at both giving as well as receiving pleasure. If you're planning on dedicating yourself to her magnificence, you'll need to do the same.

You can start off by becoming mindful of every sensation you encounter, and think of how you can use it to either pleasure yourself or your lover. Whether you're rolling out dough, bathing yourself, inhaling the sweet-smelling skin of a baby, smoothing out your sheets, riding your bike on a bumpy road, putting lotion on your arms and legs, or savouring a piece of velvety chocolate, you can take all those non-sexual experiences and use them to expand your repertoire of sensual moves.

Playfulness and sensuality are the ultimate antidotes to self-doubt and self-deprecation. They can never co-exist in the same container, and they ensure that desire always outweighs doubt, should it start to rear its ugly head.

Knowing that, if I ever start to slip into those negative zones, I immediately make a U-turn and go right back to what my inner goddess demands of me – reconnecting with my desire, soul and sensuality.

I close my eyes and listen to a salacious song or a hot movie scene, to let my imagination go wild, read poetry by Rumi or Octavio Paz, or watch a movie like Mira Nair's *Kama Sutra*, that teaches eroticism the way courtesans learned it – a lost art that definitely provides an edge. Point being, there's no shortage of ways of turning yourself on, and others with you – sure beats turning yourself or others off.

So why not create anticipation and enthusiasm to feed desire, which in turn excites the inner goddess into becoming even more erotic. She revels in knowing that her lovers adore her come-hither inviting nature. Most women wait for men to make the first move; not her.

Take charge, pay attention to your longing, research desire itself, study what your lover craves (if you have one), and create a sanctum of earthly delights.

As I studied desire myself, I discovered that timing has a lot to do with it, just like poetry and comedy. If you give into it too soon, you haven't built up enough erotic tension; if you wait too long, it loses its flavour – or worse, causes resentment when it never leads to anything – so don't tease if you don't intend to please.

Teasing is great at unleashing the imagination, but without a shot at gaining the prize, it can get boring and grow old real fast. Nobody likes a cock tease who has no intention of delivering what she promises.

If you don't intend to deliver, better stick with flirting, since it's just playful fun, without any promises or serious intention. The only agenda behind flirting is, making both parties feel good.

I used to take this beautiful long drive on a winding road, every single Friday. At the bottom of the road was a traffic light. The same homeless guy sat there week after week, on his makeshift chair. Since the light was always red whenever I got there, I'd give him my spare change. We saw each other every single Friday, so we started to say hello.

One day, he was so distraught that his head hung down and he didn't even look up. I flirtatiously said, "Hey, we gotta stop meeting like this, because people are starting to talk." Both him and I knew that I wasn't trying to pick him up with my cheesy line, I was just acknowledging him as a normal human being, down on his luck. He got up, with tears welling up in his eyes, reached into his cup, took out a couple of bucks, and said, "Thanks for making me feel like a regular guy who mattered – please buy yourself a drink on me." Of course I didn't take his money, but what we both left each other with was, a beautiful moment encapsulated in good feelings.

And that's all that flirting is – just a moment in time that's meant to make both parties feel good – something that the goddess has mastered to an art form. But since it's a lost art nowadays, I've dedicated an entire chapter to it, so stay tuned.

Let the world be your playground, and every sensual act a service to your inner sex goddess. Be mindful. Every time you make love, invest in the other person as if it's your first time together, and invest in yourself as if it's your last, so you can be fully present to satisfy that hunger in both directions. Don't ever take any part of that for granted; make it special with the right mindset, *every single time.*

Giacomo Casanova was neither attractive, nor rich or powerful, yet he could have any woman he wanted – including nuns – at a time when those things were strictly forbidden. His secret? He always planned the evening like he was going to propose; to him, he was, "something far more delicious than marriage" as he put it. And he did it *every single time.*

If you genuinely hunger for someone and want to ravish them, most people wouldn't be able to resist being the object of your desire, particularly if you show them how badly you want them.

17

But most doesn't mean everyone, so you must never push when the other party is either disinterested or unavailable. Besides, why would you want to pursue someone who doesn't want you anyways?

When a woman is turned on, she can catch anyone's gaze and mesmerize them. She walks slowly and deliberately, she stops time, she savours every moment, because her sensuality is her heart and soul. No one dare rush her; why would they want to, because they're enjoying the experience of her. And that's the essence of a sensual goddess.

But you need to awaken her and then create the best version of yourself with her help, even if it feels hard.

Performing artist Luba captures the idea of women being made not born, in her famous song, *let it go*. Some of her lyrics go as follows:

We are made, we are not born

Let it go, let it go, let it free your body and move your soul

Uniformity conventionality is the fate of our existence

Keep it safely at a distance

Let your hair down, let it free your rhythm

Let it go, let it go, let it free your body and move your soul

Scary as that process of being made and remade might feel, have faith in the fact that females were designed to constantly re-invent themselves – just look at our monthly cycles, life cycles, pregnancy, childbirth, and motherhood. Sometimes that means we might have to go through painful stuff, but there's always a brand-new phase on the other side; we were created to manage that. So trust your resilience and welcome the process of constant renewal; let your fear go, and free your body and move your soul.

Both of my childbirths were really complicated, but I still went au naturelle, so the pain was excruciating – even the docs thought I was crazy for putting myself through that. But when they placed those babies on my chest and we made eye contact, it was love at first sight.

I'd do it again in a heartbeat if I could, to give life, because it's in our design to strike that perfect balance between strong and gentle. I've always had faith in that, in various life circumstances; I couldn't have survived without it.

It all comes down to perspective, which determines how we respond to different experiences. Even under the most difficult of circumstances, life is as hard as we make it; trust me, I've survived situations that I wouldn't wish upon the worst of mankind.

The word perspective comes from the Latin word *perspicere*, which means, 'to see through', and Webster's Dictionary defines it as 'a particular attitude toward or way of regarding something'. All this is to say, we determine the meaning we attribute to something, which can be contingent upon context. Allow me to share the story of the tuna sandwich with you.

The broadcasting industry is drenched with a lot of eclectic people, with a host of eccentric experiences. The producer for my talk show was no different; he'd travelled far and wide and eaten in some of the most exquisite restaurants in the world, since he was a foodie.

One day, we were discussing the most memorable meal that each one of us had ever had. When it was his turn, he said, "A god-awful tuna sandwich, made out of canned tuna, with way too much mayo, on stale bread."

Needless to say we were all shocked. I asked him to provide context. He shared that a while back he'd been hospitalized for several weeks, recovering from major surgery. The first few weeks he was "fed" through an IV, then he was switched over to clear fluids, Jell-O after that, and eventually he was allowed his first solid meal – a "god-awful tuna sandwich on a hospital tray". As he recalled how good it felt, he was salivating, and his eyes closed in an orgasmic way. I could practically taste his experience, as he relived it.

Since then, I've shared that story many times with people who settle for so little in their relationships, savouring the crumbs that feel like a life-saving meal. And every time I do, people invariably say, "OMG that person is my tuna sandwich." At that point, I encourage them to put things into perspective, if they want more than just settling for crumbs, which will not sustain them over the long haul.

In my own life, being cognizant of realities, and picking and choosing what's healthiest for myself, has saved me from a lot of heartache, that could've easily made me lose my rhythm.

A case in point: one of my relationships started off with a big bang and then quickly slipped into a constant flip-flop between joy and frustration, pleasure and pain. I tried to constantly adapt to keep up with the other party's rhythm. Regardless, there came that cataclysmic moment when the person broke my heart, with a total disregard for my feelings.

I started to slip into that dark place where you spend way too much time wallowing in the company of sappy heartbreak music. Since that was *so* not me, it wasn't long before I decided to take charge of my life and get back on track, because I believe that happiness is a choice, just like misery.

Then, when I least expected it, the person returned into my life. I sold myself on the idea that everyone deserves a second chance, especially since I felt that relationship had the potential for greatness. So I let him back in, after telling him how selfishly he'd acted, and how the rejection had really stung. I'd hoped that would keep him from doing that to me again. And if I'm really honest, a part of my bravado also had to do with the fact that deep down I knew that I could move on if I had to, because I didn't *need* him, I just *wanted* him. FYI, most people appreciate being wanted versus being needed, to fulfil a specific function.

In any case, as to be expected, the flip flopped over to the other side once more, and I had a choice to make. Dare I put my heart at risk yet again, since the fun part was so intoxicating?

My inner goddess must've made the decision for me, because I realized that I'd already grieved him, and my heart was no longer saving the best seat in the house for him. I chose not to let him back in and moved on, knowing full well that the tide was going to turn again and again, if I allowed it.

Sadly, a lot of women remain stuck in that cycle, because they say when it's good it's really good, knowing full well that the opposite is also true. As in, when it's bad it's really bad – their heart gets crushed, they become undone, and they accumulate frequent crier points, while they expect their friends to listen to the same old stories and help them figure out why it happened yet again, versus why *they* allowed it.

If this resonates for you, and you're thinking *I get that intellectually, but my heart doesn't seem to get it,* it's because your conscious mind can't communicate with your subconscious mind – aka your "heart" which is only able to perceive the world through the five senses, not an internal dialogue. So you have to communicate with it in the right way, using a sensory channel, like sound.

The best way to do that is by making an audio recording on you smart phone, of what you wanna say to that emotional vampire, right after they rip your heart out. Express yourself exactly the way you would if you could let it all out, without fear. Next, you need to listen to it, out loud, again and again, particularly if you're considering getting back together with them.

You'll be amazed at what happens when you remind your subconscious mind of how that toxic individual has repeatedly made you feel, in a way that it can absorb it, because that's where all the big decisions are made. Trust me, I've used this method myself and recommended it to hundreds of my clients, with great results. So I want to equip you with this valuable tool.

Besides, your smart phone won't get pissed off at you if it has to listen to you complain again and again, unlike your friends who'll eventually get tired of it and wanna break up with you themselves.

At the end of the day, we always have a choice. We can take the linear route from pain to grief to freedom, or stay stuck in the cycle where we keep circling back to the pain, wasting copious amounts of time waiting for a glimpse of the freedom, hoping for possible excitement. Ultimately, adrenalin is adrenalin – good or bad – and it keeps us hooked.

My life has dealt me a lot of trauma over the years, but I've always grown from it and came out renewed on the other side, ready to take on the world, more connected to my core and spirituality than ever before. Being a psychotherapist, I've seen that magic in other women as well.

In my experience, while most of my male clients entering the second phase of their life worry about it being downhill from there onwards, most women feel the best is yet to come, because they've learned to grow a scintilla of hope into a major vision. In fact, they get a second wind to do what they always wanted to do. It's in all of you, so when your inner goddess nudges you, listen to her!

The second wind is our reward for all that we do to create and raise families, or cater to those around us in other ways, because our progesterone – the maternal hormone – plummets like crazy as we enter that second phase of our lives. Obviously, it's in our design to focus on ourselves after putting our milestones to rest.

Women who ensure that they don't lose sight of their core and continuously celebrate the sex goddess alongside the pursuit of other things, maintain their sex drive for when they arrive at that glorious stage, because the more we engage in sex, the more we crave it. So make sure that you keep your juices flowing, to become a sexually seasoned woman, when you get to the other side. It'll make your entire journey fruitful and delightful.

Being disconnected from your feminine energy will only rob you of your *joie de vie*, and leave you feeling dead at your core. At that point, too many women lose hope and start making excuses for being stuck, often blaming others.

This isn't about others; it's about *you*! Never give up control over your life by playing the victim and blaming others. That won't change the tide to make you happy; it'll only make you increasingly *un*happy and miserable, if you choose to stay stuck there.

If you think you might be stuck, shift your focus and bring your attention and energy back to what you can do for yourself, to change what you can – i.e. the future.

Many women have asked me how I keep going with such sharp focus, while squeezing every last drop of pleasure out of life along the way. In fact, some have actually started off a session by telling me that they want to be exactly like me, when I ask them what brings them in.

I explain to them that it's in all of us to be resilient and joyful, but all too often we allow the world to discourage us, and we give our power away. It leads us to think that we're not good enough, we don't fit in, people are rejecting us, our losses have beat us down. Never accept defeat, don't ever blame others for your problems; just focus on what you want, and don't stop until you get it!

Pain can be a gift – it allows us to appreciate what others might take for granted, because they have no comparison point. Moving through pain, coming out at the other end stronger than ever, and reconnecting with our desires and longings allows us to love harder than everybody else, because we're not afraid of our deep emotions. And that deep and passionate love can capture hearts and connect us to our lovers in the most magical and profound way – the way that we were meant to. So thank the universe for the pain which opened you up to be born again and come to life, with a brand new start, full of joy, confidence, sensuality, and hope!

All you have to do now is, commit to becoming unstoppable when it comes to your dreams! I've created what I call "10 commandments" for getting there; allow me to share them with you.

10 Commandments for Creating a Fulfilling Life

1.   Do whatever it takes to let go of what makes you miserable, so you can be free to pursue what makes you happy! How we feel depends upon what we focus on!

2.   Henry Ford said, "Whether you think you can or you can't, you're right!" So believe that you can, and you'll be able to make it happen!

3.   If it's worth pursuing, it'll likely feel risky or scary. Think of ships – they're safest in the harbour, but they weren't

made for that, so they venture out – embrace your own adventure!

4.   We end up with what we think we deserve. If you want more, believe that you're worth more!

5.   Time and energy are precious. Ask yourself if you're investing in what you want to grow, with interest, or if you're wasting your resources on what makes you unhappy, stuck in rumination?

6.   If you want to change how you feel, whose permission are you waiting for, when all you need is your own!

7.   Be at least as invested in yourself as the person who sucks up most of your energy!

8.   If you don't pursue your dreams, life can end up feeling like a nightmare.

9.   A purpose driven life will always find fulfillment; it doesn't settle for roadblocks, it finds detours and U-turns to stay on track. And it's never scared of asking for directions, when it feels lost.

10.   As the saying goes:

Dance like no one's watching

Sing like no one's listening

Live each day like it's your last!

I hope you're open to what comes next, because it'll fire you up beyond your wildest dreams! Your hormones will be coursing through your veins like a teenager, so you'll feel fearless, self-indulgent, and entitled to move to your own rhythm. And you'll relish savouring and being savoured by your lovers!

2: Embracing the Goddess Heart & Soul

Every March, tens of thousands of women the world over recite Eve Ensler's *Vagina Monologues*, to raise funds for women's shelters. A few years ago, I had the privilege of being invited to participate.

Being a major advocate for the cause, I was beyond thrilled. Doing it in a way that honours vaginas took my excitement off the charts. I practically had goose bumps, even though I wished they were called the "Pussy Dialogues", since by definition, a vagina is just the anatomical canal that leads to the uterus.

Now don't get me wrong, I am in complete awe of the uterus for creating life, and the vagina for making it possible – from start to finish. But when we refer to our girly parts as vaginas, we exclude the vulva – made up of all those external parts that bring us joy and pleasure, and connect us to the divine. So personally, I prefer the word "pussy" any day, since it's a powerful life-force as well as the seat of eroticism, both of which capture the spirit of the inner goddess!

In any case, the universe must've heard my cry, because I was asked to recite the pivotal piece, "Reclaiming Cunt", that connected the painful monologues to the rapturous ones. I was expected to bring up the atmosphere from tears to laughter, without being disrespectful to the former, while paving the way for the latter.

And I had to eliminate the pejorative meaning attached to the word "cunt". High expectations, I know, but I always love a challenge, especially one that fires up my passion!

27

The dialogues were already established – we weren't allowed to change a single word – and the cast was set in place. Cindy Williams (Shirley from the sitcom *Laverne & Shirley)* introduced the first set, and Joyce DeWitt (Janis from the sitcom *Three's Company*) the latter. When it was my turn to connect the two, I walked out to center stage, with black leotards, thigh-high red-leather boots, a sexy red boa, grabbed my pussy, and said "I love my cunt", in keeping with the dialogue I was to deliver.

Neither Cindy nor Joyce had practiced with me before, so this was our first time presenting together – no dress rehearsal. Cindy's jaw dropped, Joyce's eyes lit up with mischief, and the audience started like Cindy and ended up like Joyce, when I had them doing a cheer – gimme a C-U-N-T etc. I highly recommend that each and every one of you read the book, to join in!

The point of my story: pussies can and must be liberated, since they're the heart and soul of the inner goddess, and thereby our gateway to connecting with our sensuality and divine power! Without that connection, we're hollow. As such, pussies shouldn't just be spoken of as victims, or some hidden asset that men are after; one that can be doled out as needed, but not too generously, lest it become cheap and lose its value. Nor should they be referred to as just an anatomical part with nothing sensual attached to it.

Women who refer to their pussy as a vagina aren't usually on good terms with the pleasure part; women who call it pussy, put pleasure first and foremost, but not in a pornographic way that denigrates female sexuality – they do it in a way that celebrates it, the way our inner goddess demands.

Many moons ago, I wrote for a romance imprint that couldn't even acknowledge that we have a pussy. The hottest a scene was allowed to get was, him "indulging the area between her legs". It always conjured up a smoothie image for me, like a Barbie doll – an *area* versus specific *parts*. So I decided to refer to the clit as a soldier, and the lips as gates of paradise in my next novel; as in, "there stood her soldier, fully erect, guarding her gates of paradise". And her lover had to make the soldier happy to be let in. Everyone was shocked and appalled, but the novel had already gone to print by then.

Not only did women – yes, including romance writers – get excited by it, they wanted more. So I was invited to teach the local chapter of Romance Writers of America the art of cranking up the heat, using euphemisms. I got creative with things such as, "there lay her juicy split fruit, displaying its desire to be partaken of". The women in the group confessed that the class gave them goosebumps, and made "their area" wet with anticipation.

Point being, we have delightful parts; if we don't name them, acknowledge them, take care of them, make them happy, we'll be neglecting the crown jewel of our erotic energy.

If you want to experience true pleasure and allow your sensual goddess to manifest herself, you must first accept and delight in your pussy and the cornucopia of earthly delights she has to offer.

If you're not there just yet, here are some healthy tidbits to at least get you thinking about her magnificence.

When our pussies take us to that rapturous state of ecstasy, we release a lot of feel good chemicals – oxytocin, dopamine, serotonin, prolactin, endorphins, and the lining in our blood vessels releases large amounts of nitric oxide, the uber-neurotransmitter that balances everything out, so we don't need drugs. I'm getting giddy just thinking about the pleasure lab between my legs, that supplies good feelings to the rest of my body. I don't need illicit drugs to get there, just connecting with the goddess within me, who'll hook me up.

If the idea still doesn't appeal to the religious amongst you, think again. God didn't create the perfect man and woman and then ask some evil force to slap on the genitalia.

The female genitals, from the sumptuous lips to the Almighty Clitoris, are all about pleasure, unlike the multi-functional penis, with its four-thousand nerve endings to our eight-thousand in the clitoral head alone. Clearly, this gem was created strictly for our enjoyment, so it needs to be embraced for its divine purpose.

If God had wanted us to fly, we would've been given wings; but look at what we were given instead. So, let no man or woman say that women weren't intended to be sexual, because it's in our DNA, thus our birthright!

Sadly, according to anthropologist Helen Fischer, author of *Why We Love*, who's done extensive research into the human sexual make-up, "Being a human who is sexual, who is allowed to be sexual, is a freedom accorded by society much more readily to males than to females." How sad is that?

So why is the pussy undermined, despite being the gateway to all those delightful benefits?

To honour the pussy is to honour feminine energy, responsible for sensuality, nurturing, daydreaming, peacefulness, deep emotions, and giving life – none of which are geared towards ego, capitalism, and the competitiveness that drive us to produce more and more. The problem with that is, we end up working harder and harder, perpetually entrapped on a treadmill that doesn't give us a chance to stop and smell the roses. The end result: we become depleted, anxious, depressed; our relationships suffer; we can neither enjoy peace nor excitement, so we turn to addictions and other unhealthy habits to numb out.

Funny enough, when I get to that place where I'm taking on more and more, jam-packing my days like a human-doing versus a human-being, people say you've got "big dick energy", and they stop seeing me as the sensual woman I profess to be. It's a sign for me to step back, reconnect with my core, and become more present to the sensual goddess within, who feels delicious, erotic, drenched in playfulness and longing. Neither men nor women find me threatening at that point. I love my life in that state, and wouldn't trade it for anyone else's.

FYI, the masculine and the feminine energies have nothing to do with biological gender – we all have both, and we get to choose which one to put in the driver's seat, at any given time.

The goddess at the heart of feminine energy is dedicated to connecting our passion to our desire. If we suppress or neglect our desires, our passion gets redirected into hurt, anger, resentment, making us pursue happiness in bottomless pits that can never deliver. But following our heart's desire will energize us to pursue our dreams, even when we're scared, or being discouraged by the world!

Feeling ashamed of our desires suppresses sumptuous parts of ourselves, so we feel empty, lost, unhappy, dissatisfied. But if we honour our desires, our heart will follow – and you know what happens when we follow that heart!

But before you can unleash your inner goddess and her desires, you have to honour the pussy for fuelling her with delight, sensuality, fun, mischievousness, deliciousness, pleasure, not as something dirty, that's judged by external criteria that torment the rest of you. It starts there and then flows out to the rest of the body, like warm, velvety rain on a parched soul. From there, it can flow out to other women, awakening the goddesses within them, each time you treat them as one. It truly is a life-changing experience for both parties when one touches another's soul.

I can't tell you how many times I've had the privilege of seeing a woman come into her own and blossom, after feeling like a *persona non grata* her entire life, because of my *genuine* love and faith in her. Watching her transform beyond who she thought she could ever be, gives us both the greatest joy, and we grow together.

Encouraging and uplifting each other to celebrate being feminine is a truly powerful feeling! But we can't fill another if we ourselves feel depleted or empty, so we need to intentionally tap into our inner source every single day, to have surplus for others!

Being a goddess isn't a game, just to get what we want; it's a *daily* practice, an *intentional* way of living, a *constant* turn-on – not to be turned off when it's inconvenient. It's about being your best self! Every step should reflect that. And when it does, every sidewalk will become your catwalk, because you'll be flaunting your feminine energy, with pep and swagger in your stride.

Feminine energy is a beautiful thing, embedded in loving ourselves and our bodies, and knowing the worth of all women the world over. The best way to stifle it is by hoarding it, or tearing other women down – which is just plain ugly. We are thus called to mindfully encourage, support, and build each other up, to create a *tour de force*.

Naomi Wolf stated in her book, **The Beauty Myth**:

"A consequence of female self-love is that the woman grows convinced of her social worth. Her love for her body will be unqualified, which is the basis of female identification. If a woman loves her own body, she doesn't grudge what other women do with theirs; if she loves femaleness, she champions its rights."

If you're still with me, celebrate your commitment to self-love by treating yourself to the ultimate date, just like you'd plan for someone you were trying to seduce. Create the ultimate feast for your *all* of your senses – it's the equivalent of having a balanced diet. Build the right ambiance, prepare your favourite food and drink, have a sensual bath, slip into something sexy, light some candles, spoil yourself with a gift, put on your favourite music, dance, and lay it on thick with everything you like about yourself – brag, show off, give and receive compliments without restraint!

Feel better? How does your pussy feel? Does she feel sexy? What does she want in this moment? Don't be afraid to caress her, respond to her longing, touch her lips as you'd like yours to be kissed – soft, gentle and feathery; or strong, deep and wet. Close your eyes and enjoy feeling alive! And if you wish to end the evening with rapturous sex, go for some *ménage à moi*.

Once you're done, open up those peepers, seductively look at yourself in the mirror, and start repeating "I am divine and delicious!" over and over again – bet you'll end up smiling and feeling gorgeous, naughty, even powerful! Follow up by telling yourself what you wish to hear from a lover; *you don't have to rely on someone else to hear those words*!

And that's just the beginning, not an isolated date. Make your environment decadent, buy yourself fresh flowers, be ready for more impromptu dates with yourself, or with a lover. Your home needs to be suitable for a goddess to inhabit, imbued with sensual delights everywhere you turn.

One of my professors, Francesca Gentille, a truly sensual goddess, hosts various webinars from her sumptuous home. I can't wait to be invited into her delicious surroundings, since they speak volumes about her decadent sensuality, from rich colours to soft candles, rare artifacts to bejewelled cushions – a bordello couldn't convey a more welcoming atmosphere.

Being immersed in sensuality awakens the mind to new adventures, and it can turn you on even when you're not feeling good about yourself. But you have to learn to connect with the powerhouse between your legs, without holding back, if you're to take yourself to new heights.

Our ancestors acknowledged the pussy as a mystical, sacred power, since it gave life, could lead to crimes of passion and wars in a heartbeat, or make one lose their mind and make irrational decisions. So, several centuries ago, they decided to honour it by assigning it a symbol – a pictorial representation of the pussy itself.

But then, as the patriarchal society took over, it decided to disempower it, by making that symbol represent a heart instead, even though it doesn't look anything like it. It's about time that we reclaim it. So the next time you see that symbol, put your hand on your pussy, and promise never to neglect her again – it'll be like a secret society handshake, that acknowledges a dedication to the work that needs to be done to release sensual goddesses the world over.

I love acknowledging mine, by having conversations with her. When life gets too crazy, I stop and ask her, "Hey Sexy, what do you think we should do?" She invariably tells me to slow down, chill out, and refocus on my feminine energy.

At that point, my body becomes highly attuned to my senses, and I feel electricity running through me, turning on every cell in my body, demanding a pussy party versus a pity party.

Even a sexy conversation can give me a visceral experience in that moment – one that tugs on the cord that connects my heart to my pussy, making it pulsate, twitch, and throb with anticipation, anchored in my lascivious imagination. The whole thing practically gives me an orgasm, thanks to a sensory overload which takes me to ecstasy, without a single touch, because that's what feminine energy can do.

If you want that experience, I encourage you to liberate the seat of your femininity – your pussy. Get her out of her panties, go commando, give her a name, talk to her, listen to her, let her breathe, and never ever let her be shamed, by yourself or another.

I physically liberated mine quite by accident. Anyone who knows me well, knows that I prefer to spend my money on delectable experiences before things. I'd rather take a decadent vacation than buy an expensive bag; invest in super-sexy underthings and lingerie than super-expensive clothes that don't touch my skin.

One day, when I went to buy a delicious yet expensive bra and panty set, I couldn't afford both. But instead of downscaling to something not as sumptuous, I bought just the bra and decided to return for the panties at a future date – what can I say, my girls needed support.

Going commando felt so good that I never did return for those, or buy any more panties in the future for that matter. My pussy has always thanked me for that – i.e., not being constrained for no good reason.

Going sans panties also improved my posture, particularly in short skirts. It's time to unleash yours – instead of waiting for casual Fridays, go for panty-less Mondays, so you can actually look forward to them, in a celebratory TGIM way!

What we decide to put on our bodies can have a huge impact on how we feel. You wanna feel sexy, put on something sexy or take off something unsexy. You feel like garbage, put on a garbage bag and see how quickly you'll wanna get out of it. Point being, do whatever it takes to feel good about yourself!

To find out where your work lies, test your GQ – Goddess Quotient!

GQ Test

1. What did my mother teach me about being a woman?

2. Was I celebrated for being a female, or constricted and put down?

3. What does being a woman mean to me today?

4. Have I learned to suppress my feminine energy, or celebrate it?

5. How do I feel about my body?

6. How do I feel about my pussy – do I carry shame in her, or do I honour her for the magnificent, powerful, life-giving, pleasurable creature that she is?

7. On a scale of 1-10 how much do I enjoy being a woman?

8. On a scale of 1-10 how much do I enjoy having a pussy?

9. What turns me on? Do I know my body's capacity to experience pleasure?

10. What turns my pussy on?

11. What turns me off?

12. What turns my pussy off?

13. Do I feel sensual or uptight?

14. How have my lovers described me?

15. Do I feel connected to my inner goddess or disconnected from her?

16. What am I doing to celebrate and sustain my feminine energy?

17. Do I know how to pleasure my pussy?

18. Can I teach a lover how to treat me right?

19. Can I teach a lover how to treat my pussy?

20. Who are my female role models – the goddesses I wish to emulate?

The answers in your GQ test should tell you what you need to work on. The good news: we can all get there, even if we have to work through trauma, brainwashing, and everything else that's tried to take our vital force away from us – our negative chatter for one.

The following exercise will help you identify your negative chatter and move past it. It's truly critical to cleanse that clutter, because it takes up a lot of space, and it constantly drains our creative and sensual energy. Think of it as a clean up, to create space for your beautiful new thought process.

Challenging Your Negative Chatter

1. For the next week, at the end of each waking hour (or as often as you can), jot down your negative self-dialogue, particularly things that you'd never say to another human being. For example, "I'm such an idiot!"

2. Identify and jot down the belief that likely led to that thought.

3. Give yourself the permission to be human and make mistakes.

4. Challenge that belief by saying something positive about yourself – brag if you can – especially in the area of self-doubt that led to that negative chatter in the first place.

I've dedicated an entire section to challenging your negative chatter, since it's a must, if we're to clear the space for the goddess to do her work. So stay tuned.

Once you accept yourself as a flawed, fun, fantastic human being, you'll switch gears to enter your fabulous side!

All you have to do now is, give yourself the permission to honour the source of your feminine energy – your pussy – because she was created to fill your life with all sorts of earthly delights, in the most sensual ways possible!

Get to know her, love her, celebrate her, and most important of all, listen to her. She always knows what's best for you, and innately wants to protect you and your birthright to be a sumptuous goddess.

3: Getting in Touch with My Pussy Power

We often hear people say that men have two brains, but enough blood for only one to function properly at any given time. And if they have to choose between the two, they generally think from their little brain. But while we may not talk about women having two brains, we most certainly do. The only difference is, we don't always listen to the little one, even though we should.

For example, if we don't feel safe, or if we haven't sorted out through our trauma, even though *we* may not have the voice to say "no" to sex, pussy can clamp shut to protect us. Or if we're unhappy in a relationship, feeling resentful towards our partner, or sex is no good, pussy causes pain to stop us.

Then there are those moments, where late at night, or in a desolate parking lot, pussy tells us that she isn't feeling safe, especially if someone is gaining on us. Sadly, we don't always listen to her, because we don't want the other person to be insulted by us running, because it implies we think they're creepy or dangerous. In hindsight, we wish we'd listened to her – every single time – because she doesn't try to talk us in and out of stuff, she just listens to the gut instinct that's there to protect us.

Over-thinking in your head can give you analysis paralysis. Thinking from your pussy is like checking in with your inner sensual goddess. As such, when I have to choose between heads and tails, I always pick tails – hasn't let me down yet.

The relationship you have with your pussy is one of the most important relationships, because it reflects your relationship with yourself. It decides sensual or shameful, alive or disengaged, dangerous or safe, enchanting and spellbound or timid and invisible, pleasure driven or performance driven, and so on.

Point being, pay attention to her; she's smarter than you think, and more in touch with your gut instinct and feminine essence than you realize. More so than anyone else on the planet. So never ever put anyone else in charge of how you feel about yourself!

A woman once called me up and asked if I offered any workshops for her to "get it right?"

I asked her, "Get what right?"

She responded, "You know, the whole nine yards, from feeling sexy to doing sexy things ... because the last time I tried to dress up in some sexy lingerie and please my man, he told me to stop, because I looked like a ridiculous whore!"

Appalled, I inquired, "What did you do?"

She said, "I stopped and ran out of the room ... why, what would you have done?"

I told her, I'd stop and leave the room as well, but only after telling him, "If that's how you feel, I'll take my business elsewhere."

We both laughed and acknowledged the importance of always staying in touch with our inner goddess. If someone tries to kill her spirit, we need to get as far away from them as possible!

Your pussy is the spirit of your sensual goddess, so really connect with her.

Connecting with Your Pussy

Let's have a pussy dialogue right now; as in, if your pussy could talk, what would she say? Really connect with your second brain and tell her story – share her desires, hopes, dreams, fears – it's time she spoke up! Don't be shy. You can use a pussy puppet, mould a pussy out of clay or dough, look in the mirror, tell a friend, or simply write it down. You'll be amazed at what you'll learn about her, and how she likes to be treated just like the rest of you – with love, attention, affection, acceptance, feeling like a priority.

If you shame your pussy, put her down, neglect her, or don't appreciate her, she'll shut down. But if you acknowledge her, praise her, pamper her, worship her, take your time with her, she'll open up in exciting ways like you never imagined; and she'll want to return the favour in infinitely delightful ways. Isn't that how most women work in general?

The reverse is also true. If a woman is uptight, her pussy is likely uptight. But if she revels in her sensuality – she's the woman who walks into a room with delicious written all over her – she's likely playful and delectable in bed.

Now I'm not talking about a woman's physical appearance; I'm talking about her attitude, mind-set, confidence, body language, how she carries herself. I've known many stunning women who take hours dressing up to perfection, but still remain self-critical and completely lack umph.

Personally, I love identifying with Gloria Steinem's sentiment:

I pray for the courage

To walk naked

At any age

To wear red and purple,

To be unladylike,

Inappropriate

Scandalous and incorrect

To the very end.

A woman who is connected with the goddess within her, without exception, not only honours her own sensuality but also knows how to make others feel good about theirs. She's warm, friendly, doesn't put others down, and she's never seen as a threat. Both men and women enjoy being around her, and the generous way that she upholds and celebrates others. To know her is to love her, and be loved by her.

A sensual goddess is intimately connected to both her mind as well as all five of her senses, so she can turn herself on in multiple ways, using both her brains. In fact, you don't even need to touch her pussy for her to experience an orgy of sensations. She'll hear her lover's voice, make eye contact with someone across the room who's mesmerized by her, get a whiff of a familiar scent, or simply savour a chocolate covered strawberry, and her pussy will become aroused, because she's squirming at the thought of all the exciting possibilities. Her crowning jewel is visual, tactile, auditory, olfactory and gustatory – boy is it ever, because she enjoys the taste of sex!

Speaking of sex, it's never just about getting off for her; it's about savouring each moment, connecting with herself and/or her partner, and about a tsunami of endless waves of pleasure that energize her to keep going.

Beyond that, the pussy brain can control the goddess's moods, depending upon where she is in her cycle. She likely has three mindsets – internal, external, carnal.

Internal: 3-5 days before ovulation, a woman can go internal and become contemplative

External: 5-7 days before her period, a woman can go external, where she lets you know exactly how she's feeling

Carnal: During ovulation and throughout her period, she has huge cravings – if she's not getting sex, she's hitting up the carbs

FYI, the pussy brain is as complex as the pussy body. So let's get acquainted with the rest of her, because more women know what their pussy *doesn't* want, than what she wants and craves. And let's face it, if you don't know how to satisfy her cravings, the sex goddess she fuels starts to lose her luster.

The Ins and Outs of the Pussy

Just like it's many delightful functions, the pussy has many delightful parts, which pleasure her in myriad ways; but most women haven't bothered to get to know them. They spend more time taking care of their hair, nails, and skin, than taking care of their pussies, and then they wonder why they still don't feel sexy. Pussy is the seat of sexy, get to know her and indulge her, and you'll feel sexier than all the other stuff combined.

Allow me to give you a little tour around your pussy right now. I'd like you to be an active participant, so whip out that mirror to identify the special landmarks on your treasure hunt, versus just having me talk about them, like the tour-guide that drones on versus letting you experience and savour each moment.

Mons Veneris – pubic mound

Labia Majora – thick, protective, outer lips

Labia Minora – thin, sensitive, inner lips

Glans – aka the clitoral head – the top left quadrant is the most sensitive and can give an hour-long orgasm if touched just so, using a method designed by Dr. Victor Baranco, founder of the More University, geared towards sexual arts

Crura – two legs that run from the clitoris towards the urethra like a wishbone (you won't be able to see those, but it's important to know where they lay, all the same)

Prepuce – clitoral hood that protects the head (female equivalent of the male foreskin)

Commissure – supersensitive lining inside the prepuce

Urethra – urinary canal (you can only see the opening)

U Spot – the area just below the clitoris and above the vaginal opening that hugs the hidden parts of the clitoris, making it ultra-sensitive.

Clitoral Bulbs – spongy padding that lies between the crura and the urethra (again, you won't be able to see those)

G Spot – it's an area rather than a structure, that sits 2-3 inches inside the vagina, on the tummy side (when unaroused, it's dime-size and flat, when aroused, it's spongy and silver-dollar size, and makes you feel like you have to pee)

Anterior Fornix Erotic Zone – aka the AFE zone – is closer to the cervix and more sensitive than the G-spot (hence it requires lighter strokes than the stronger, come-hither strokes that reach the G-spot just so), and it can provide a *cul-de-sac* orgasm

Vagina – the outer third is the most sensitive part, and similar in size to the ultra-sensitive penis head; it's also the part that grips to hold on tight, while the inner two-thirds balloons to accommodate all sizes (but only if you take your time with foreplay)

Vulva – the *piece de resistance* comprised of all of the above external parts, like an orchestra versus a single instrument, combing the best of abilities, just waiting for a talented conductor to create pure magic

Now that you know the key players, let's get you into a rhythm to dance with these exquisite creatures.

Pussy Workout

1. Start breathing deeply – pretend you have a balloon inside your belly that's being blown up big and then deflated completely. Watch your belly go up and down.

2. Now imagine yourself drawing breath from your pelvis, pulling it up right through your body, and then out through your mouth.

3. Throw in some pelvic action. As you pretend to draw each breath from your pelvis, tilt your hips forward and squeeze your PC muscle as tight and as pulled up as you can, then swing back and release as you breathe out. (The PC muscle is the same muscle that you squeeze and release when you hold or release your pee.)

This can also be done by laying on your back in a comfortable position – knees up, feet down flat. When you do it on the bed/ground, tilt your hips to a comfortable tension while you tighten up, and push your back down as far as it will go as you release.

4. Keep the pumping rhythm going. Be sure that your breathing is synchronized with the pumping motion – breathe in with the forward hip thrust, while squeezing you PC muscle as hard as you can; breath out when you tilt your hips backwards, releasing your PC muscle.

5. Once this rhythm becomes second nature to you, train that PC muscle to move like the wave in a belly dancer's belly. Practice a one-two-three move where you squeeze three times, pulling up higher and higher each time, almost like you're rhythmically sucking up a ping-pong ball. My portmanteau for that exercise is grip-tease, because it can grip and tease like nothing anyone ever imagined. If you want to add another motion during intercourse, do some figure eights with your hips

in female dominant positions, and stop at the knot to do a grip-tease.

6. Add some noise – moaning/groaning on your outward breath. It will enhance the much-needed oxygen flow, while communicating excitement.

7. When you do this privately, take off your clothes, and run your hand across your pussy – not touching it, just hovering about an inch above it. You'll likely feel some heat, almost like what you'd feel from your hand over a gently heated stove.

8. As you examine the magnificent powerhouse between your legs in a mirror, let your fingers open up the petals on that gorgeous orchid, and watch its lips get poutier and poutier, as its hues change – pink to fuchsia to purple, mocha to caramel to chocolate, shellacked in a glistening sheen from getting wet. Notice other changes in your pussy, as she becomes more and more aroused, and possibly pulsates.

9. Now experiment with different types of moves:

- up-down stroke

- side-to-side stroke, paying attention to the 2 o'clock and 10 o'clock marks on either side of the clitoral head

- gentle roll of the clitoral head between your forefinger and thumb, exercising no more pressure than if you were trying to write with a ball point pen, without denting the paper; most men use twice the pressure than what a woman enjoys (their penis has half the nerve endings so they assume a woman requires the same amount of pressure)

- circular moves

- figure eights

- massaging the entire erogenous zone with your fingers held together

- opening up your lips with one hand, while the other gently and barely taps against the clit

- putting pressure with the heal of your palm on the mons, while you fingers drop down to play with your clitoris and lips

- taking your time with the top left quadrant of your clitoral head, with light feathery moves (stroked just right, it can give you the longest orgasms)

- using a vibrator, while you keep the rhythm going as you pump up against the vibrating head

- using a pulsator like the womanizer (it feels like a mix between suction and pulsation) – documented as the most effective treatment for women with orgasmic difficulties, and menopausal women complaining of lowered intensity (trust me, my lips never lie)

OMWORK with a Partner

OMWORK is Orgasm Meditation, based on the method designed by Dr. Victor Baranco. If you engage in this practice regularly, using the following steps offered by OneTaste.us, you can have hour long orgasms. So I encourage you to check out their demo clips on YouTube, for delightful instructions to open yourself up to the ultimate orgasms.

1. Set aside uninterrupted time, and invite your partner to join you. There needs to be a lot of trust between the two of you for this to work!

2. Prepare the space. Your nest should include a floor mat or mattress, several pillows, a firm cushion for him to sit on, a hand towel, gloves (optional), water-based lube, and a timer.

3. Get close and comfortable. You need to be naked from the waist down, but you can leave your top on; your partner stays fully clothed.

4. During the practice, your partner needs to inform you of every step they're going to take before taking it, allow you a chance to communicate how you feel about it, and listen to your requests and feedback.

5. The 15 min meditation should start and end with your partner applying grounding pressure on your thighs and calves, using a nice messaging touch.

6. After the initial grounding, your partner should apply a nickel size lube on their left stroking finger and their right thumb. Following that, they need to rest their right palm under your butt, letting the right left thumb to rest on your introitus – the entrance point on your pussy.

7. Your partner can then start stroking in a way where they can *feel* the strokes rather than trying to make anything specific happen. The strokes should be short, gentle, and s-l-o-w – if they think they're going slowly, they need to go slower still, and even slower after that – applying light pressure as one would apply if they were to gently touch their eyelids.

8. After a while, your partner needs to slow down their touch even more, using even slower, broader, downward strokes for two minutes.

9. At the fifteen-minute mark (from the start), your partner should put their hands broadly across your pussy and push down firmly, until it feels good for you and ultimately grounds both of you for the rest of the day.

10. The hand towel can be used to remove any excess lube and then folded to reveal the clean side, which is then placed on your pussy.

11. The session ends by both of you sharing a moment where you felt something in your own body. For instance, many partners share that they felt heat in their finger that shot like electricity through their entire body.

When we don't share after the fact, we miss out on the intimacy that comes from learning each other's desires. I didn't realize how important that was until a lover started to ask me what I liked the most about each experience, and shared what turned his crank and rocked his boat.

It's like reliving the moment, reinforcing the best parts, and then making a mental note of something that can be intentionally built upon in the future. And the more detail the better, utilizing all five senses, to make it a truly sens-ual experience that penetrates through to the core. For example, "I love the taste and texture of your juicy lips" versus "You have nice lips".

To get an even better understanding into your pussy, for expanding your sensual enjoyment, do some homework on your own. Grab a copy of my friend Carlyle Jansen's book, "Sex Yourself". If you need detailed visual instruction for stimulation, invest in Dr. Betty Dodson's video on "Self Loving" and learn to love yourself in the most delightful ways possible. You will need to keep at it for at least an hour the first time, to really get to know yourself, in terms of what feels good and what doesn't.

When we increase our enjoyment and engagement, we increase our partner's enjoyment and engagement, particularly if our partner is a male, because nothing turns a man on like a turned on woman!

It's a delightful dance between wanting, aching, achieving satiety – only to create more hunger – back to the first step. But it takes dedication to make it a priority, not fit it in as an afterthought, like a chore that has been neglected far too long.

It all starts with us – a ladies first sport if you may – from knowing what we want, to communicating it in ways that fulfil our craving.

If *you* don't know what feels good for you, how can you expect your partner to know; but if you sample a buffet of possibilities, you can teach your partner how to indulge you with a host of delightful, delicious, erotic flavours. And the more creativity you bring to the process, the more connectivity you'll create.

Most people have one or two ways of making themselves come. Being content, they have no desire to see what might work better, feel more intense, etc..

But your body gets bored of experiencing the same sensations over and over again, not to mention misses out on a lot more, simply because you didn't dare to try out new things. You wouldn't keep your car radio tuned to the same two songs, would you? Why do that to your inner goddess, when you know that she loves a variety of music, remixes of her favourite songs, and singing along in a primal way – screaming with delight.

Once you have some tricks up your sleeve, make a weekly date with yourself or your lover, to nourish both your brain as well as your body with one additional sexual treat each week – be it a new fantasy/role play, a new sexual variation, or a new sexual purchase (movie, book, toy, lingerie, sexy board game, something to get you excited about trying out your new purchase). Of course, if you can lead up to it with a sumptuous buildup, your inner sensual goddess will thank you all the more, and reward you with earth-shattering experiences that'll transport you into another orbit.

But even beyond the sheer pleasure of it, when you fully embrace your sexuality and the power within it, you'll unleash your sexual power – a close cousin to your pussy power – in all its magnificent glory.

Pussy power is about yourself, sexual power is defined by your interactions with others.

Our sexuality can be the container of greatest joy or sorrow, pain or pleasure, depending upon how powerful or powerless it makes us feel. It can present itself in simple ways, like sex appeal giving one an upper hand; or complex interactions, involving titillating sex scandals or painful sexual trauma.

But like it or not, this powerful force that's become the synecdoche for myriad things – used to sell anything from libations to cars – exercises it's omnipotent influence in most aspects of our lives, on a daily basis. And it's a lot more convoluted than we realize, because the same stimulus can impact people in different ways.

For example: a woman with body image issues may become unglued and turned off by Victoria's Secret commercials; a sex addict may get sexually triggered and aroused by the same, to the point of losing all control.

Sexual power can titillate without touching, using erotic energy that exudes a tsunami of sexual tension that's greater than the physical build up before a genital orgasm. It's what dances upon the spectrum of power play between "yes" and "no", drenched with possibilities. Small wonder our vitality depends upon this force, explaining why people give into it at a risk to all that they are and all that they have.

From boardrooms to bedrooms, no other force can manipulate our thought processes like sexual power can – many a nation has been led to war, many powerhouses brought to their knees.

A case in point: Lady Diana, Princess of Wales, looked like a porcelain doll, adored by the world. But Prince Charles risked all to be with Camilla Parker Bowles for the intimacy he experienced with her. He indicated that he'd remained faithful to Princess Diana until their marriage was irretrievably broken down. Rumour has it that his scandalous affair with Camilla was as charged as the affair between her great grandmother and his great grandfather, and powerful enough to survive four decades of drama – everything from dismantling of royal marriages to outrageous tabloids, and ultimately tragedy.

Dr. Catherine Hakim, a renowned sociologist and author of *Honey Money: The Power of Erotic Capital*, refers to sexual power as erotic capital. According to Dr. Hakim:

"Erotic capital combines beauty, sex appeal, liveliness, a talent for dressing well, charm, social skills, and sexual competence. And rather than degrading those who employ it, erotic capital represents a powerful and potentially equalizing tool – one that we scorn only to our detriment."

Hakim believes the reason some people seem to lead charmed lives – people want to be around them, doors open up for them – is because of the power of erotic capital, the overlooked human asset that is at the heart of how we work, interact, succeed and conduct our relationships. She feels that it's just as influential in our lives as riches, education, and connections.

Seeing that our culture is becoming more and more sexualized, the importance of erotic capital will only continue to grow; which in turn will change the role of women in society – since they have more sexual power than men – revolutionizing the power structures in almost everything we do.

Thus, we need to give ourselves the permission to embrace the phenomenon that's very much at play in every facet of our lives, so we can work with it instead of having it work against us.

Embrace the goddess within you, and she'll ensure that you maintain both your passion and power. Commit to loving the body she resides in, and it'll work with you versus against you.

4: Loving and Accepting My Body

Sexiness is never about what your body looks like; it's about you owning whatever body you have, and running with it – i.e., a mindset versus an appearance.

It's about loving your body and allowing your inner goddess to do the rest. It's about being grateful for good health. It's about doing whatever you need to do to feel good about yourself and then projecting that confidence onto others.

As Sophia Loren put it, *"Sex appeal is 50% what you got, and 50% what they think you got."*

When we claim our beauty, the entire world follows suit.

Sadly, most women project their insecurities versus the deliciousness of being a woman, because they loathe their bodies instead of delighting in them. Being a psychotherapist, I have a front row seat to how destructive that is.

I have a constant stream of women coming into my office who are unaware of their sensuality. They're more fixated upon what they *don't* like about their bodies versus what they *do* like, since they're invested in the fabricated myths that the media projects, where sex appeal is all about numbers – quantified for easy saleability – from age, to weight, to measurements of different body parts.

All of that puts some of them in a state of constant self-recrimination.

What they don't realize is that they've become paralyzed by that, and are unable to dance to their own rhythm.

They stop noticing how their captivating smiles, curves, wiggles, laughter, and various body parts – from their painted toenails to their tousled white hair – are working their magic on those who surround them. If only they could see the likes of my friend CoCo La Crème bringing down the house with her luscious curves, during one of her burlesque performances! She owns every part of her body with great confidence and allows the goddess to do the rest. You can see her delicious sensuality drip out of her, captivating men and women alike.

But most women's fears make their world really small, where they're stuck between being expected to look their best, trying to enhance their looks to meet that standard, and then being made to feel superficial, by the same people who started the cycle in the first place.

Over time, the mixed messages attack their self-esteem in the worst way imaginable – they're damned if they do, and damned it they don't. Thus, many women end up joining the masses and start judging other women by their looks, more harshly than any judges they'd want to face themselves. And that just tears apart the sisterhood and destroys the feminine energy where we can all come together to change the world.

The biggest culprit in this cycle is what the media falsely endorses, as the normative standard for sex appeal, when Ogi Oggas and Sai Gaddam's book *A Billion Wicked Thoughts* has demonstrated that the majority doesn't necessarily agree with that standard.

Combining online behavioural data with cutting edge neuroscience, they uncovered startling truths to make just that point, via findings which included facts like, men prefer overweight women to underweight women; men often seek erotic videos featuring women in their 50s and 60s; and so on. But since that's not what the media promotes, most women are completely unaware of it, and become distressed by feeling that they don't have what it takes to have sex appeal.

So why exactly does the media do that to us? One of the main reasons is to sell us goods. I took a marketing class that I dropped on the very first day, because I learned that it's all about making people feel bad about themselves, so advertisers can sell them remedies. And the easiest way to make someone feel bad is by setting unrealistic, *quantifiable* gold standards that everyone aspires to, that can never be met.

If those numbers had any merit, they'd be programmed into our biology, and thereby consistent across cultures and millennia, but that simply isn't true. Thus, the best thing that we can do for ourselves is to not buy into any of it, and take back control, so we can feel good about who we are, *as* we are. Our inner goddess doesn't give a damn about all that other stuff. All we have to do is, love ourselves and live authentically, with her in the driver's seat, since she knows what's best for us.

Ignoring our sensuality and giving into what the media pushes is really costly to us, because it chokes our natural desires and instincts. The sad part is, we're so deeply immersed in that ideology that we don't even notice it. But we can recognize it in our best friend when she feels bad about herself for no good reason. In fact, we find it so egregious that we try to do whatever it takes to pull her out of it, since we recognize how dangerous that can be to her psyche.

We can see value in women close to us that we often can't see in ourselves, because we get used to the climate we're raised in, bit by bit. I could always fight for the underdog but rarely for myself, because I didn't even realize that I was in trouble.

Us not noticing the slow brainwashing is analogous to what happens to a frog. If it's placed in a pot of water which is set to boil, it'll just stay there, even as it's boiling, since it continues to adapt to its life-threatening environment. But if you were to try to put it into boiling water from the outside, it would recognize the danger and not go anywhere near it.

It's time to fight those constraints that shame us for how we look, what we feel, what we desire, and embrace the beauty that lives within us. And it has to start with impressionable little girls, before those influences start to take hold.

If Barbie were real, she couldn't walk, she's have to crawl, thanks to her proportions. Yet, that's one of the first symbols we present to little girls – a standard they'll likely aspire to one day.

Small wonder eating disorders are devouring more and more girls, at younger and younger ages.

And if that isn't bad enough, they're also being bombarded by fairy tales where females wait to be rescued by Prince Charming, with no desires, courage, or goals of their own – they'd rather sleep for a hundred years versus pursuing their own goals.

And when Prince Charming does come along, he doesn't meet the criteria that've been placed on him either, to meet *all* of his princess's needs – be a good provider, a romantic soulmate, an engaged father, exceptional lover, emotional guru, someone who makes her happy, and someone who manages to pull his weight around the house, and then some.

Since it isn't remotely realistic or possible for any one person to do all that, many women end up being disappointed and unhappy with their partner, believing that there's something wrong with him, because he's constantly failing them by falling short.

Even where Snow White is surrounded by *seven* men, who could easily team up to take care of the above seven needs, she identifies them by their moods and lives to service them. Personally, I'd pick *getting* serviced any day, especially under those circumstances, picking and choosing the one that suits *my* mood at the time!

Tragically, all those influences cause women to become disconnected from reality, especially their own needs, desires, sensuality, and all the other delights that their inner goddess wants to bestow upon them, including pussy power!

Dorothy Black who studies female sexuality, captures the sentiment exquisitely:

"Turns out, the story that's been packaged and sold to us about our bodies, desires and sex drive – as fact – might have been more than just a little bit influenced by that creepy old man in the corner called patriarchy.

This is nothing new to subcultures that still venerate and nurture female sexual energy as a force to be reckoned with. My first experience of this was with Shakti Malan, a now world-renowned tantrika who runs workshops showing women how to tap into their desire and 'drop into' their own bodies.

If you're wondering what other bodies we've collectively dropped into, just open any women's glossy and take a look at what your sexual power is being sold to you as: demure, made-up, withholding, brittle with frailty and in stasis, waiting to satisfy The One."

Denying those false and/or controversial messages, and embracing what is, is the spirit in which your inner sensual goddess can manifest herself. Her heart and soul know what you truly desire, and are committed to helping you get it and live life on your own terms, with contentment, in your juicy, delicious, sensuous body, which just wants to revel in its feminine energy.

But it takes a conscious effort to love your body exactly the way it is. Until I learned to do that, even I bought into those erroneous, media-generated images and messages.

I'd often find myself breathless, heart pounding, going white-knuckled around my Diet Coke, as I witnessed a familiar scenario – different drama series, different players, but the same sequence. Their eyes meet, words are barely exchanged, and next thing you know they're ravishing each other with urgency, against a wall/door, atop a desk/counter, gyrating their perfectly sculpted bodies like gymnasts, with flawless choreographed moves, until they coalesce into a hot and sweaty simultaneous orgasm, and then melt into each other's arms, spent and satiated. It always managed to make me feel like I was wasn't enough, or I was missing something, even though I should've known better, since I work in the media and I'm privy to all that goes into every *perfect* second of each and every *perfect* production.

It must be because my otherwise cerebral brain got repeatedly hijacked to its reptilian side, with its visceral thinking – media counts on just that. So I often found myself wanting to have my bod look like that, so I could strut it confidently, and cause a tsunami of excitement just like those unrealistic bodies.

Eventually, I learned that what Sophia Loren had said was in fact true. When I learned to get comfortable in my own skin, and project confidence in my sex appeal, I too could turn heads with my ordinary bod.

A case in point: one time, I accompanied my friend David Menzies – a columnist for various major publications – to the Toronto Auto Show, to comment on the sex appeal of various cars and trucks. I had my "power suit" on – a sexy little number – and managed to turn quite a few heads, because I walked around as if I owned the place, since Menzies had arranged for a special media pass to photograph me near cars which cost more than the average home. Watching everyone's reaction, he said, "I just went from feeling like a big shot for having you *with* me, to wanting to *be* you, so I can experience your sexual power."

Sex appeal starts from within and then dances with whatever comes in its path, including the body it resides in. Having a cosmetically enhanced body won't do it in and of itself, regardless of what the media preaches, to proselytize the masses to it's unrelenting religion.

When we learn to love our bodies, accept our sensuality, embrace our sexuality, and allow the desires in our pussies to emerge, our sensual goddess appears. And when she does, we become freer and happier, our lovers become more delighted, and our relationships reach nirvana.

But when we withhold, either because we don't accept our bodies and their desires, or because we try to appear coy since we've been taught that's what women are supposed to do, our sensuality literally leaves us. At that point, if we're in a relationship and our partner wants to be intimate with us, the coyness and "humility" don't make us appear more desirable; they destroy our shot at the magic that happens when we surrender to reckless abandon.

In the worst-case scenario, it could lead to an affair. While I'm not condoning affairs and the pain they cause in any shape or form, I'd be remiss if I didn't shed some light on the most common scenario I repeatedly come across, so it can be prevented.

John – a fictitious, composite character – has a withholding wife. So he tries to come up with creative ways to engage her sexually. He uses everything from his charm, to back-rubs, to doing more than his share of chores, to candlelit dinners, all to entice her.

At first, he feels that he has the power to seduce like the infamous Casanova, even though he might be clueless around some basic psychological principles. But with time, he realizes that his pleas for touch fall on deaf ears, because she will be intimate with him only when *she* feels he's earned it, because *together*, they've set up conditional intimacy.

What follows is, the seduction turns into begging and eventually arguments, making John look less and less attractive to his partner. And if that isn't enough of a beating for his sagging ego, the sting of constant rejection and his wife's counter attacks are sure to get to him.

Eventually, John will feel powerless and thus stop making advances altogether, which is bound to make him feel unhappy, and possibly angry, resulting in the disintegration of his sexually diminished relationship. At that point, if someone starts to give John attention, he'll likely be too hungry to resist, so he may devour the adulation.

When we fall in love, it's very much a mirror-mirror-on-the-wall situation, since our amour reflects back only the good in us, making us feel like we're the fairest of all. But when that stops – i.e., our partner starts to reflect our bad parts and ignore the good parts – the proverbial mirror is shattered, bringing bad luck to the relationship.

John may thus start to feel entitled to pursue the opportunity that's glaring him in the face. Most affairs start when one stops feeling special at home, and someone outside the home makes them the center of their universe. It's just too irresistible to pass that up under those circumstances.

Again, in no way am I exonerating affairs, implying that all affairs happen for those reasons, or suggesting that it's the partner's fault, but it happens that way often enough for me to feel compelled to comment on it. It's reality, not something I invented.

Ironically, a lot of women worry about someone out there who's prettier than them jeopardizing their relationship, when the threat lives right between their own ears; or for that matter, between their own sheets.

If you want your relationship to be hot and sexy, make it happen. If you love your relationship but don't enjoy sex, come up with a mutually respectful solution that protects it and keeps it viable.

In other words, stop worrying about women out there, and start listening to your inner goddess. Not only will she help you love your body and embrace your sensuality, she'll give you the confidence to honor what you want; whether it involves more sex, less sex, or no sex, with or without a partner. It's that simple!

I'd like you to try out a body mapping exercise right now to connect with your body, because most of us aren't even fully aware of what our body feels.

Body Mapping Exercise

Draw two outlines of the female body – front and back – and duplicate them for the two exercises that follow. The first one will help you connect with your body, the second one with your sexuality.

Take the first pair of outlines and use traffic light colours to highlight the body parts you love in green, the parts you're unsure about in yellow, and the parts you loathe in red. Do this for your front and back, and write a brief description that speaks to why you feel the way you do, beside each part.

Do the same with the second pair of outlines, to designate your erogenous zones in green, where you need some time and trust before being touched in yellow, and the off limits areas in red.

Beside each area, write out a brief description that speaks to why you feel the way you do.

Once you've done that, I want you to really process where those attitudes started. Was it something someone said, something you experienced via media, something you were applauded or bullied for, a trauma that your body is storing?

For the unhealthy and painful attitudes, you'll need to work with a professional to restore good mental health. Your inner goddess won't settle for anything less.

A woman who loves her body and the feminine energy it contains is comfortable in her skin and enjoys life to the fullest. There is no limit to what she can do to fulfil her dreams and desires. She thinks big, so she is big! And she's courageous, often outrageous, and definitely confident enough to share the secret to her self-assuredness with other women. In a world where females can loathe captivating women and underhandedly cut each other, she passionately converts them to her way of thinking – being responsive to the inner goddess and reaping the benefits.

Why is she so generous? Because she feels there's enough fun to be had by everyone, in any size, form, shape, ethnicity, or orientation, so she doesn't believe in hoarding anything. In fact, she draws everyone to herself and her resourcefulness, with an irresistible gravitational pull. Women want to be her, men want to be with her.

Oscar-winning actress, Charlize Theron, appreciates the magic of dressing up in sexy clothing. So she enjoys all the free garments that the fashion industry bestows upon her, giving her "a really nice closet" that she and her girlfriends call "Narnia". Theron gives some of those sensual pieces to her friends. She believes that since she can't wear everything, she should share her good fortune with others, so they too can feel sexy. And that's what a true sisterhood veteran does – she nurtures other women's sense of self and sensuality, versus hoarding it for herself, like an insecure creature.

I can't tell you how much joy I get when I can give my clothes to other women who truly enjoy receiving them and wear them with pride. They say they'd never have the guts to buy those provocative pieces for themselves, but when it's a gift they dare to give it a shot, and invariably love how sexy it makes them feel.

Being a goddess is a potent cocktail of attitude, generosity, owning and working what you've got, and also not being afraid of letting your sensuality emanate like the essence of your pheromones.

And if you happen to feel good enough to rock a hot outfit with stockings and come-fuck-me stilettos – regardless of your age or shape – or wear red lipstick brazenly, all the better. But only for your own sake, not because you feel pressured by someone else, which would put your power in *their* hands.

When you reclaim your power, awaken your sensual goddess, and start to feel delicious again, you'll save your feminine energy to do delightful things, versus wasting it on being someone you're not, and then hating your life because of it.

It's all about enjoying yourself, without the unnecessary limitations that we tend to place on ourselves. If you're self-critical, the lack of joy is coming from that, not from how you look.

On the flipside, imagine how life could be different, if you looked beautiful in a media-esque way. Would you have more fun, go out on more dates, walk more confidently, have more sex, enjoy yourself more?

What's stopping you from doing all that just as you are?

Beauty has nothing to do with it. I've known many models who lack confidence, who aren't having lots of sex, and who're certainly not enjoying life or having more fun – they move food around on their plates versus actually eating it, they keep long hours, they have to go home early to get their beauty sleep, and they're under a lot of pressure to look a certain way. And their dates aren't about being in a romantic bubble, or cocooning on the couch, enjoying each other; they're all about being displayed, with a very short shelf life.

I know a lovely woman who was a supermodel in her youth. She said men just wanted to be with her to show her off, or to sleep with her; women wanted to be with her to get her leftovers. Her biggest fantasy was to gain a lot of weight or have her face get disfigured in an accident, so she could see who was for real. Ultimately, she quit before she was asked to, because she hated the life she was living – it wasn't fun by any means!

There's a lot of freedom in not holding yourself up to impossible standards, or worrying about what others think. I can attest to that personally, because being a TV host can garner a lot of hate mail. People have been brutal about my looks and asked me how I could allow myself to be seen on TV. It doesn't bother me because I don't let it. I just feel sorry for any woman who has to do that to another woman, to feel better about herself – and I doubt it that she succeeds.

The most critical part of the equation is, honouring your body versus rejecting it. When you reject your body you hurt yourself, because it's a crime against yourself, one that you pay a heavy price for.

Allow me to end this chapter by quoting two women, who eloquently capture that spirit of embracing and loving your body *exactly as it is*.

Sex Therapist Alexandra Katehakis, author of **Erotic Intelligence**, says:

"Bodily ideals, although diverging wildly in different cultures and periods, challenge and judge every individual – even the seemingly 'beautiful'. While such aesthetic standards can encourage healthy self-improvement, they often impair self-acceptance. We have constant proof of our corporeal failings – and of our inevitably temporary and comparative successes. An exalted, unrealistic sense of one's bodily perfection cannot substitute for a realistic, healthy body image. ... We're all built into bodies that have innumerable socially unacceptable realities like susceptibility to illness, elimination, and deterioration, to name only a few. To deny any aspect of your actual body and functions is to cut yourself off from life and reality. ... How can you separate your identity from your body, and show your body as much kindness and compassion as you might show an honoured guest? If you aim to grow your psychological capacity for healthy relationships, learning to love your body unconditionally is a good place to start – after all, you're rather attached to it!"

If we don't love and enjoy our bodies, we can't possibly love and enjoy the sexual power they emanate. But if we can embrace every last bit of ourselves, we can generate the most powerful form of sexual energy, which can propel us in the direction we want to pursue, to go wherever we want to go.

Author, Mistress Singing Deer, couldn't have put it better in **Brazen Femme**:

"When we lock away parts of ourselves we believe to be shameful, unacceptable or unlovable based on the messages we get from the world around us, we become fractured, split. When those 'unlovable' parts remain hidden away in the shadows, we

are not whole, and if we deny the complexity of what we are, we're walking around with only a portion of our power. We're not all that we can be in the world."

Accept all parts of yourself. Don't feel bad about the stretch marks that indicate that you brought life into this world – think of all the women who'd trade their body with yours in a heartbeat, just to be able to have the privilege of creating a new life.

Don't reject scars, which show that you survived a major illness. Don't reject wrinkles that show that you've come this far despite life's challenges.

It is my sincerest hope that you love your bodies exactly as they are, and allow the deliciousness in them to emanate, sans any barriers.

But just in case you have any residual negative messages still lurking around in your head, let's free up your mind next, from all the clutter that can take away from you loving yourself to the max, and enjoying your newfound freedom!

5: Freeing My Mind

The biggest thing that blocks us from being who we are and living life on our own terms, is the negative chatter in our head.

So, I felt compelled to write this chapter to address all that junk once and for all, so we can clear out the space to dance to our own tune. If you're already there, feel free to skip ahead and dance your way to getting your sexy on, in the next chapter.

But if there's chaos in your head because you're at a war with yourself, it's due to an incongruence between your inner and outer self – i.e., your authentic self versus your outward persona – and we know which side always wins *that* battle.

What makes it even more complicated is, your inner self has a dark side, known as the shadow – a side that's essential for our existence, but we're made to feel ashamed for having it, so we hide it.

How does that incongruence happen in the first place?

When we're kids, we learn to suppress major parts of ourselves to adapt to our parents, since it's in our best interest.

But 96% of families are flawed or dysfunctional to varying degrees, so even though that adaptation may have helped us survive as kids, it doesn't serve us as adults.

If anything, it leads to a split self that's constantly at war with itself, causing insurmountable anxiety, among other things. So we need to break those old beliefs and thought patterns that caused us to become fragmented.

The greatest source of our anxiety is the expectations we place on ourselves, based in erroneous beliefs and perfectionistic standards. FYI, perfectionism programs the brain to constantly be on edge, with strict black and white thinking.

So, we need to put away the measuring sticks that make us feel inadequate, embrace our imperfections, and foster the courage to pursue our dreams, just as we are. At that point, the sky's the limit with respect to what our inner goddess can help us accomplish, because her sole destiny is to put us in charge of our own life, so we can move to our own rhythm, in the most fun and sensual way possible.

Don't be afraid of confronting your demons; your inner goddess will help you sleigh them, and then place the reigns of your life back in your hands. And that's where the fun adventure begins, when your inner and outer selves become congruent, and you embrace your shadow, because all parts team together at that point, to fulfil your heart's delectable desires.

Let's begin by identifying and removing the negative chatter in your head, so your authentic self can emerge.

Think of it as de-weeding your garden to let those flowers grow. We'll then move into understanding how your shadow fits in, and bring everything together, so your heart, soul, and pussy are on the same page.

Identifying and Challenging the Negative Chatter

Complete each column on the next page, to get an inventory of those negative voices/thoughts in your head, where they came from, how they can be challenged, and the new messages that'll replace them.

Negative message in my head	Whose voice is it?	How can I challenge that voice?	New Message
Eg: I'll never amount to anything	Eg: Mom's	Eg: Mom did nothing major with her life, but I love what I do	Eg: I love who I am. I'm not defined by that message any more

Once you've sorted through all that, you can have a temper tantrum like a child, on the floor, complete with moving your arms and legs. It pushes the anger and negative energy out of your body.

Should those negative thoughts rear their ugly head ever again, replace the word "I" in "I am ..." with your own name – studies show that that makes it much harder for us to be self critical.

I used to call myself an idiot, every time I made a mistake.

When I replaced "I'm such an idiot" with "Rebecca's such an idiot" I found myself defending myself in third person, pointing out all the reasons that I wasn't an idiot. Try it out for yourself right now, with your most frequently used negative phrase.

You're now ready to embrace your shadow, which is the other part that puts up roadblocks.

The Shadow Self

The shadow represents the characteristics that are deeply hidden within us, because society disapproves of those, even though they're necessary for various reasons. For example, selfishness, lust, greed, anger, rage, hatred, manipulation, seductiveness, a need to control, and so on. But although those traits are generally hidden from others, it is extremely important for us to know and accept our own shadow. Deepak Chopra says:

We are all aware of having dark impulses, which include hatred, fear, and aggression. These impulses arise from the unconscious, and our normal response is to keep them there. We push the dark side out of sight, yet it doesn't go away. It seeks expression, as all energies will.

Carl Jung identified three important archetypes: *the Persona, the Shadow,* and *the Self.* He posits:

Good does not become better by being exaggerated, but worse (as is the case with us wanting more and more); and a small evil becomes a big one through being disregarded and repressed (e.g. resentment). The Shadow is very much a part of human nature – it's only at night that shadows disappear. To become conscious of it, involves recognizing the dark aspects of the personality as very present and real. This act is essential for any kind of self-knowledge – and knowledge is power.

The Self: The Self is the most important archetype. It is called the *"midpoint of the personality"* a center *between consciousness and unconsciousness.* It signifies the harmony and balance between the various opposing qualities that make up the psyche.

The Persona: The persona is the mask we wear to make a particular impression on others; *it may reveal and conceal our real nature.* It is called an *artificial personality* that is a compromise between a person's real individuality and society's expectations – usually society's demands take precedence. It is made up of things such as professional titles, roles, and habits of social behavior. It serves to both guarantee social order as well as protect the individual's private life.

The Shadow: The shadow is at the crux of self-realization, when one recognizes and integrates it. It is the "negative" or underdeveloped side of the personality.

The Shadow is *made up of all the reprehensible characteristics that each of us wishes to deny.* These *repressed characteristics* of the psyche become dissociated from one's conscious life.

The further out of awareness The Shadow is, the blacker and denser it becomes; consequently, the greater the need to project its "wicked" content outward and onto others.

To gain congruence, we must invite the 'shadow self' back into our awareness, acknowledge its legitimate right to exist, and send a clear message that it will no longer be ignored or rejected.

Understanding darkness gives light its context and meaning. But in order to do that, we need to identify our shadow first and foremost.

Identifying My Shadow

Bring to mind a person you don't like very much, possibly even hate. Write down a thorough description of that person, specifically capturing those traits and qualities about this person that you don't like.

Draw a box around what you have written. Label the box, "MY Shadow."

What you have written down is that hidden part of yourself – The Shadow – the part that you have suppressed or concealed.

It may be a part that you fear, can't accept, or hate for some reason. Maybe it's a part of you that needs to be expressed or developed in some way.

Perhaps you secretly wish you could be something like that person whom you hate.

A brilliant woman in one of my classes hated the woman her husband had an affair with, for obvious reasons. When she did the above exercise, which didn't make any sense to her at first, she wrote down the woman's following traits as unconscionable: walks into a room like she owns the place, has men swooning all over her, takes whatever she wants, nothing stops her from having a good time, etc. etc..

When I asked her if she secretly envied any of those traits, she said, "All of them ... every single fucking one of them!" It was her aha moment, and she finally got the meaning behind the exercise.

One of the ways we can express that hidden part of ourselves is by being drawn to a toxic lover, or having crushes that we're too embarrassed to share. For example, a person who's overly humble and being walked all over, may envy the narcissist's ability to show off, be charming, and impress others; or a commitment-phoebe may be drawn to dismissing partners – the onus is on them to keep the relationship casual. *They're flip-sides of the same coin.*

Ask yourself, how many friends or romantic partners have you had who fit the description of your most "hated" person?

Isn't it curious how we sometimes choose these "hated" people for our close relationships?

Now take a piece of paper and write down the similarities between people you end up with, especially the traits that drive you crazy – i.e., Your Shadow. In some cases you might go out of your way to avoid those. Either way, that emotional reaction is telling you something about that hidden part of yourself, seeking expression.

Some refer to those shadow traits as dark passengers in your life – the ones you hide even from those closest to you. But whatever you do, don't hide them from yourself; they're your guests, parts of you seeking approval.

Accepting our shadow is critical to accepting our whole selves. When we do that, we no longer need to project our shadow onto others; nor do we need to be drawn to those who have the courage to express *their* shadow, so we can vicariously express those parts of ourselves. The latter is especially dangerous since it makes us hold onto relationships that cause turmoil in us, because letting go of those would mean abandoning those parts of ourselves that we find unacceptable, thereby creating a split self. Congruence encourages a stronger sense of the self, and an acceptance of the real self, by us and others, without shame or self recrimination!

Write out what dis-acknowledging those parts costs you, and your pussy. For example, hiding selfishness may be keeping you from fulfilling your desires, fear might be keeping you from dreaming big, rage might be using up a lot of your emotional energy, ignoring hedonism, lust and seductiveness might be downright torturing your pussy – need I say more?

Furthermore, suppressed desires lead to resentment, anger, and all kinds of non-goddess behaviours, that irk the pussy, because they keep her from getting off!

In order for you to feel whole, you need to embrace *all* parts of yourself and find harmony between them, so your inner and outer selves can stop duelling over your inner goddess.

I invite you to accept Your Shadow as a part of yourself; even welcome her as a gift when you need that driving force. At that point, you'll be able to hear your desires, your pussy's desires, and all other urges crying out to you that you tend to suppress; plus, you'll have the drive and the energy to fulfil them. And that's where the fun begins!

You truly are a treasure – if you don't treasure yourself, no one else will either.

Now embrace that sassy, courageous, unstoppable goddess, in all her sensual glory, without anyone or anything taking away from any of that. Drop the *shoulds* and replace them with *wants*, so you can chase your dreams, unapologetically!

You go Girl, because you got game. Don't let anyone tell you otherwise! Time to get your sexy on!

6: Getting My Sexy On

One of my favourite TV shows of all times was *How to Look Good Naked* – the British version. The host would start off by asking the main candidate for each show to come out in her underwear, and place herself in a lineup of nine people, in the spot that she felt she belonged in, with respect to her looks.

Each candidate would invariably insert herself in a much lower position than where she belonged, based on audience ratings. Then, when he'd tell her how much higher she was actually rated, relative to other women in the lineup, the woman would be shocked, every single time. But it didn't shock me one single bit, because I know from firsthand experience that women tend to be the hardest on themselves.

What really impressed me about the host was, he never went to the places where most women go. Meaning, he didn't once talk about what the woman felt were her negative features; nor did he try to change those like a typical makeover show would. He only built upon what he thought was worth showing off. You'd never hear him tell a woman how she could hide this or fix that; you only heard him tell her how to play up what she liked about her body, and flaunt what he felt needed to be shown off.

By the end of the show, the woman's attitude and confidence would change so much that she'd be willing to walk on a runway in her underwear, with underwear models no less. He wouldn't quit until he helped her get there, just as she was.

I'd always get edge-of-my-seat excited to see the mental transformations. The show wasn't about physical makeovers, pegging people against each other, or giving roses to some and rejecting others. The show was about making each woman enjoy her assets and accept everything else with a great deal of confidence.

Before you can even think about seducing anyone, you must seduce yourself first, with self-acceptance (who you are), self-exploration (what you like), and sexual confidence (what you can do). It will provide the ideal foundation and backdrop for everything else, not to mention open up possibilities beyond anything you ever imagined. From sure-fire seduction to mind-blowing orgasms, uber intimacy to ultimate connection, it always begins with you owning it, working it, loving it ... and of course your pussy power.

Sexiness in not about the body you have or what your body looks like; sexiness is about the attitude you have towards the body you got, and what it can do, once it learns to get comfortable in it's own skin. If you're constantly worried about your looks, you'll disable yourself from being fully present in the moment.

A recent study involving 26,000 women, showed that the single factor that's most responsible for women's sexual inhibitions is, their insecurity around their physical appearance. Small wonder we reach our sexual peak later on in life, when we feel good about ourselves, not necessarily when our bodies look their best.

Interestingly, most women think about their looks as often as most guys think about sex – however fleetingly. There's absolutely no way in hell that a guy will let any insecurities around his body/looks interfere with his sex life, neither should we.

At the end of the day, be excited about who you are, and make sure others know it too. It's all about accepting yourself and projecting that sexual confidence onto others. If you need to do something to feel good about yourself or gain confidence, by all means do it; but just for your own sake.

Once you feel good about your body, mentally rehearse the experience you most desire, using visualization techniques, so you can actually anticipate the steps that will help you make it happen – from relaxation, to the right mind set, to the right moves. Athletes use this technique with startling results, so can you.

This is especially important when you're about to get it on. Be clear on what you want for yourself, to make it a meaningful experience for the both of you – don't censure yourself in any way. Bernie Zilbergeld writes in *Male Sexuality*, "Sexual messages from the brain to the genitals must be clearly sent and received. If the nervous system is obstructed, it won't send the right messages to the genitals. The most common obstructer is anxiety."

When the brain and genitals get into a fight, for women, generally the brain wins, for men, it's the genitals. The best sex requires you to be fully present emotionally, so don't let distractions ruin it for you. Just because something doesn't feel quite right in one area, doesn't mean you should allow it to overtake other areas – that's like throwing the baby out with the bath water. If anything, sex will help you feel closer at those times, by releasing Oxytocin – the stay versus stray, bonding hormone.

If you're thinking, what if I'm not in the mood? Behavioural psychologists suggest, if the feeling doesn't precede the behaviour, indulge in the behaviour anyway, focussing on how you'd like to feel versus how you are feeling, and the feeling will soon follow.

This is more important than you might realize, since with women, desire and arousal can flip-flop, so you may need to experience arousal before you can feel desire – which will eventually come, and with it the hormonal help to kick in more desire. This is why the more sex you have, the more you'll crave it; the lesser you have the lesser you'll miss it – the only way around that is by throwing yourself back into the loop of the sexual cycle.

Beyond the flip-flop, there's also discrepancy in how we get turned on in general. There are two models of sexual desire – *spontaneous desire* and *responsive desire*. In spontaneous desire, any random stimulus can turn an individual on (generally more common with men); in responsive desire, one feels like having sex after certain criteria are met, or when they start getting into some sensual acts – similar to the flip-flop that can happen for many women. Knowing how you get turned on is crucial to getting there, and to getting your sexy on.

There are also many other ways of getting your sexy on. A really fun way is via sexercise, since it allows you to sensually connect with your body in myriad ways. I never knew I had those moves in me, until I signed up for pole dancing and striptease classes.

If you're thinking, there's no way that doing a striptease will make you feel sexy – you're likelier to feel self-conscious – you're not alone. But just like playing dress-up – dress-down in this case – something magical happens when you get into it, a mental transformation of sorts. Trust me, I know what I'm talking about, because when I teach my sexuality classes, I really get into it – how else am I supposed to demonstrate that sex can be fun, imaginative, and easy to talk about?

I contort myself into positions that would make Houdini proud, and I expect my students to follow suite. And it's that very state of abandon that makes the women get caught up in a rapturous, fun moment, which ends up making them feel oh-so-sexy, like nothing they've ever felt before, because they're totally in their bodies versus their heads.

Most of them share that they never realized what their bodies could do, once they stopped worrying about their limitations. Think about how bumble bees aren't supposed to able to fly based on their bodily ratios, but they don't know that, so they fly gracefully nonetheless. Hopefully you'll have the same confidence to try out different things. Who knows, maybe you'll be confident enough to get locked up in a lewd position for the cleaning lady to find the next day; but hey, I'm willing to risk it if you are.

Now while I'm not going to spell out the details of the bump & grind, since we all like to move in different ways, I'll cover some generic tips and cool steps to get you started in Appendix A; your feminine energy and sensuality will do the rest.

But before you can even think of getting into any of that, I want you to name your pussy. You have to connect with her to get your sexy on. Without a name, she doesn't exist; you'll be like Barbie – a smoothie with nothing that distinguishes her from Ken.

When I do my workshops, we always start off with a naming ceremony. First, we go around the room sharing stripper names that we've picked out for ourselves, because it somehow seems easier to start there. Everyone has a great laugh and then we refer to each other by that name for the rest of the workshop. It's amazing to see the transformation, once the women give themselves the permission to be sexual.

Next, we name our pussies – it can't be slang or an anatomical word, it has to be something meaningful, like naming your child. I make sure they put a lot of thought into it, because they have to share why they chose that name. It always amazes me to hear what they come up with and why. From there on in, they have to pledge to refer to their pussy by the right name – in class and everywhere else after that.

The ceremony is truly a powerful ritual, because it shifts the energy from reserved and semi-nervous to full-on erotic, sensual, naughty, giggly.

79

FYI, if you do decide to strip for a lover, keep in mind that the tease is even more important than the strip, because that's what draws him in, and what shifts your attention from worrying about your body, to playing with its sensuality. My two favourite movies that've mastered the art of the tease are "*The Lover*" and "*The Piano*" – if you haven't watched them, stop everything and watch them right now.

In "*The Lover*", a wealthy man – referred to as "Chinaman" – offers a young French girl a ride to school on a daily bases. Each day, we see their hands get closer and closer together on the backseat of his luxury car, while they sit at opposite ends. After days and days, their hands finally touch, barely. It's truly an orgasmic moment, due to the build up of sexual tension. I remember the entire audience in the cinema sighing, because the scene was so sensual, even more so than the full frontal scenes that followed.

In "*The Piano*", Harvey Keitel's character helps out Holly Hunter's character with some work around her house, in exchange for listening to her playing the piano. Each day, after finishing up, he comes by and lays on the floor, while she plays. He's truly taken by her, even though she's simple, and covered up from head to toe. One day, he discovers a tiny little hole in her thick woolly stocking and becomes obsessed with seeing that little piece of flesh that he wasn't supposed to see. He eventually gets the courage to put his finger on the tiny hole. The entire cinema, full to capacity, gasped at the sensuality of the gesture, just like the scene in "*The Lover*".

Another thing that these movies had in common was, they captured the tease with ordinary, fully-covered women, because it wasn't about being naked at all; it was about the build-up.

When you attempt a striptease, you need to start off with getting your own sexy on, and then build from there. Some women have shared that they were a bit leery at first, afraid that it might feel contrived, but when they got going, it made them feel really sexy, not to mention occupy their mind completely, so it didn't hijack them to the wrong place. It's about being present in your body, versus giving into the static in your brain.

I thought I had my own mental static under control. But right after I had my hysterectomy, I realized it was hiding just beneath the surface, ready to take over.

All my girlie parts had been yanked out, so I felt like I wasn't a woman any longer. And then came the big challenge.

I had to facilitate a workshop, teaching women to love their bodies as they are. While I truly believe that all women are beautiful in different ways, I couldn't extend that grace to myself. So I started to cry because I felt like an imposter.

My son reminded me of what I said all the time: there will always be someone younger and someone older; someone prettier and someone not as pretty; someone thinner and someone more voluptuous; someone with one feature or another that we like more than our own, and someone who'd settle for our features. In other words, every part of us is on a spectrum; and since I find all women to be beautiful, regardless of where they fit in, he reminded me that I too was on that same spectrum.

I cried even harder: this time with tears of joy. He nailed it and I left to do my workshop with more confidence than ever before.

What stands in *your* way of self-love, self-acceptance, and feeling sexy? Whatever it is, find a way to get rid of it.

And while you're at it, get rid of all the unnecessary junk in your closet as well, the stuff that gets in the way of you feeling your very best.

I used to grab bargoons all the time – the kind where you think, it's not top shelf but you can't go wrong at that price – and I held on to my old clothes forever. Naturally, my closet was bursting at the seams, but most of the stuff hadn't been worn in quite a while.

One day, I decided to go shopping in my own closet. I tried everything on, and unless I absolutely loved it and felt good in it, it wasn't staying. Seventy percent of the stuff didn't make me feel sexy and my pussy just scowled at the thought of going anywhere near those unsexy things. So much so that when I checked in with her, she felt insulted and de-pussified.

I encourage you to do the same. And when you buy something new, it should be something that gets you excited, at any price, not just because it's cheap.

Next, I want you to go and buy yourself a couple of sexy underthings, the kind that make you feel mischievous. I know I said that I liberated my pussy by going panty-less, but if there was a pair of silky, crotchless panties, I'd consider them, just for the fun of it, especially if they involved lace or feathers. But they'd have to match my high heels – every girl knows that if the shoes match the outfit it completes the ensemble.

Speaking of underthings, get fitted for a proper bra. Most women buy the wrong size and it ruins their posture and shape, since it has them hunched over, spilling out all over the place.

Don't get me wrong, I'm all about spilling out, but only intentionally, not randomly. A good posture makes for a sexy, confident presentation.

Once you have your sexy underthings all sorted out, book yourself in for some boudoir photography. It'll be the best investment you'll ever make in getting your sexy on. I did my session right after getting rid of my mental static. The pictures made me look like a lingerie model ... and feel like one too.

Since then, I've suggested it to many women, in all shapes, ages, sizes, and different body types. One by one, they started to see that beauty truly is in the eyes of the beholder – the photographer in this case. They'll show you ways of looking at yourself that you never imagined before, because you were too caught up in your mental static. It's the same way that you see other lingerie models, without an awareness of *their* mental static.

Loving and accepting our bodies, and giving ourselves the permission to enjoy our sensuality and sexuality just as we are, can be a truly liberating and empowering experience. There's no better way to get your sexy on. But as with all great experiences, you need to work at it.

I encourage you to spend some time each day to enjoy your body. Look at it, indulge it to see what it likes, experiment with a new toy to push yourself past your limits – they've been around forever, or at least since Cleopatra ingeniously created the first unofficial one, taking pleasure from bees trapped within a thin-walled jar.

Since then, the first "official" one came into being in the early 1800s, when an MD couldn't keep up with the increasing demand of twiddling clitties to "cure hysteria", believed to be caused by anorgasmia – aka lack of orgasms. Had he been around in this day and age, I'm sure he would have people lining up to sacrifice themselves for an apprenticeship, because most men and some women would give their right arm to know how to get us off. And most women would love to have their pleasure acknowledged as a crucial part of mental health.

I sincerely hope that you're feeling free, exquisitely sexy, and loving who you're becoming. Time to embrace that power and fully let go! It's in you, maybe you just don't know it yet. I promise you that once you connect with it, you'll have everyone in awe, bowing down to it.

Think Daenerys Targaryen from *Game of Thrones* – once she realized that she had power within herself all along, she transformed into a woman who could get what she wanted, and she managed to propel her self-love into getting love and respect from everyone around her. Now that's power!

7: Empowerment

When a woman fully accepts herself and is in touch with her inner goddess, everything starts to come together; and she starts to live life on her own terms. She's a fun, fierce, femme, who will never act as a doormat for *anyone*!

Some may think she's acting like a bitch, because they're used to women in their life always putting them first, even at a huge cost to themselves. But a goddess knows that to be true to herself, she can't please those who don't have her best interests at heart – she'll do anything for those who do – so if she gets labeled negatively for taking care of herself, so be it!

The word "bitch" generally implies all manner of unpleasant characteristics which should have any man running. Yet, one of the most common questions I get asked by women is, "Why do men love bitches?" suggesting anything but.

As such, I decided to survey hundreds of men on this controversy, by putting it out there on a radio show I was hosting, since it was "talk radio for guys" after all. Their answers were consistent, with a running theme that indicated that it was the "bitch's" attitude toward *herself* that was attractive. They respected the fact that she held her own, and expected to be treated as an equal. So they wouldn't dare treat her as anything less, since she simply wouldn't put up with it.

It isn't any different from a bad boy's appeal – women always try harder to impress them, because they know they're not enslaved to anyone. The word bitch in this context stands for: **B**abe **I**n **T**otal **C**ontrol of **H**erself. So next time someone calls you a bitch, don't get upset. Embrace your inner bitch and invite sensuality into the mix. It'll capture the essence of the woman that biographer and novelist Elizabeth Ruth described: "Her ass is her own, until she needs a good spanking. Even then, she's nobody's slut but the slut inside ...."

Goddesses are their own gatekeepers – they choose whom and what they will and will not allow to enter their lives. In other words, they're always in the driver's seat. And they do so with utmost grace and sensuality – they never feel the need to compromise their femininity to become more competitive. They rather revel in it, so they can be a lot of fun – from boardrooms to bedrooms.

Being feminine doesn't mean being less powerful. If anything, it's quite the opposite, provided it's organic, graceful, and real. So don't be afraid of allowing your inner goddess to shine through and take charge!

A goddess defines her own ever-changing parameters. She yearns to connect, but will never be compromised or determined by that need; which is not to say that she will never compromise. But when she does, it's truly a compromise, not her becoming lesser for someone else to feel greater – she simply won't allow that.

And if something isn't working out, she isn't the least bit afraid of walking, because there's no shortage of opportunities in her world. She *never* has to chase anyone; people line up for the privilege of pursuing her, because she draws them in.

Furthermore, she will never show jealousy, or let her emotions run the show – she knows that'll only give someone power over her. If she doesn't like it, she'll deal with it in ways that don't undermine or humiliate her. She realizes that the person with the biggest reaction is the least powerful, so she stays in control. Beyond that, a goddess will always be true to herself first and foremost; the only approval she craves is that which comes from within. She believes in herself enough to make others believe in her. Wherever she goes, whatever she does, it's by choice – *her* choice – as such, she goes through life enjoying herself.

To be chosen by her as a partner is true delight, because if she lets you into her inner sanctum, you're in for a ride of a lifetime! She has being feminine down to an art-form. She can be very playful, but she doesn't play manipulative games. She has nothing to prove, so she's just as happy with winning as she is with conceding. Her sensuality is a living breathing entity, at once mysterious and explicit, and a pure joy to behold. She's no one's slave, but being a sex slave to her pussy can provide her immeasurable pleasure!

That said, in as much as she enjoys her sexuality and sensuality, there's a lot more to her than meets the eye. She's free, yet she lives by the rules that she created for herself.

So, what exactly are those "rules"? Herewith, the 10 "commandments" that guide her to stay empowered, always. But not every rule will apply to everyone, or for that matter apply in the same way all the time.

10 Commandments of Female Empowerment

1. Goddesses Hold Their Own: They're self-reliant, they can stand up for themselves, and they hold their ground. They never beg anyone for anything, least of all to be loved – how attractive is that anyways? They know that if they were to become dependent upon someone, their neediness might make them compromise their integrity. So they take care of themselves and move to their own rhythm. And if someone doesn't align with their core beliefs, or disrespects them in any way, they'll just move on, instead of allowing them to undermine them. As Eleanor Roosevelt once said, "No one can make you feel inferior without your consent."

2. Goddesses Are Financially Independent: They know the power and payoffs of being financially independent. Too many women rely on others, who end up controlling them; and when a relationship goes bad, they remain stuck. But a goddess will never find herself in that position. She enjoys her economic freedom, which gives her freedom in general, with the power to choose how she lives her life, and who she lives it with.

If she needs to be spoiled by some retail therapy, she knows that the person who pays off her credit card bill will never humiliate her by demanding an explanation. A friend of mine got carried away on her girls' night out and had a little too much to drink. Later, they all went to see a psychic, who sold her a three-thousand dollar amethyst rock, telling her that it would change her energy and chi. Drunk out of her mind, she didn't think much of it and plopped her credit card in front of the crystal ball. Next day, when she woke up, she called me with "good news and bad news". I asked her to tell me the bad news first. She shared, "I bought a fucking three-thousand dollar rock last night … not sure what I was thinking. Good news: I don't have to explain myself to anyone".

Women who take charge of their own finances refuse to control anyone else's money, or have anyone control theirs. And they expect their partners to do the same. In other words, while they don't expect to be taken care of, they certainly won't sign up for taking care of a partner either.

3. Goddesses Never Take Things Personally: They're a legend in their own minds, and make sure that they make themselves a legend in everyone else's mind as well. Someone who can't see that or has a problem with it is probably too weak to be with a goddess in the first place.

Know your value and love yourself, because until you do, you can't love anyone else or be loved by them. Never buy into anything that causes self-doubt or goes against the love you have for yourself. A goddess looks at someone's negative opinion of her as a difference of opinion on something really important – herself – just like religion and politics, and won't engage in such a discussion. If anything, she thinks of those individuals as weeds that are trying to take over her garden, so she pulls them out of her life, without taking anything personally, because she knows that 90% of put downs and rejections are based in external circumstances and internal insecurities, which cause people to tear others down. So if someone doesn't like her, she sees that as *their* problem, not hers, because she loves herself to bits and won't be defined by someone else's opinion of her.

4. Goddesses Never Set Themselves Up for Disappointment: A goddess will never have false expectations that can neither be understood nor fulfilled – it keeps her disappointment down to a minimum. This doesn't mean that she doesn't have expectations; it only means that she ensures that they're realistic and reasonable, and she's comfortable walking away from anything that's intolerable.

5. Goddesses Know How to Have a Good Time: Goddesses know how to have a good time, without becoming a good-time girl. They'll pique one's interest just enough to seal the deal, without giving anything away for no reason. That said, their own pleasure is always a good enough reason for giving it away. They generally *love* sex, and can pursue it for its own sake, or as a means to a great end. It's about pleasure for them, not performance to please another.

6. Goddesses Don't Let Guilt Run their Lives: They may feel guilt for not feeling guilty, but that's where it stops. Since they don't hold anyone responsible for their own mistakes, they don't expect to be held responsible for other people's mistakes. If something is going to make them feel bad, they simply won't go for it. But once they commit to something, they never look back with regret. Even if it doesn't work out in the end, they think of it as a lesson, not a mistake – and when was the last time you felt bad about learning a lesson? We all know what's right or wrong, we don't need guilt to nudge us. All guilt can do is stop us from living life fully and happily. Besides, most experiences are only as bad as we make them, by how we feel about them – take ego and guilt out of the picture and things don't look so bad anymore.

7. Goddesses Plan Around their Own Moods, not Others' Moods: Being people focussed, it's generally a female tendency to get bent out of shape if someone else is in a bad mood; they can think that it has something to do with them, even though they haven't done anything wrong. Regardless, they can take on responsibility and try to do whatever they can to lift the other party's spirits, and possibly feel they're inadequate otherwise.

Goddesses tell themselves, "I know he/she is in a foul mood, but since I didn't put him/her there, it's not my responsibility to fix it; so I'm going to let him/her wallow until they're ready to come around." Hard as it is, they resist the temptation to intrude and simply walk away, after offering to help. Eventually, the person comes around after fixing their own bad mood, without needing to fix any bad blood between them. Bottom line, when it's someone else's bad mood, don't make it yours.

8. Goddesses Invented the Mantra "I'm Worth It": When I was a little girl, my mother overdid the humility bit; so much so that I became an emotional cripple with no self-confidence, very early on. Relationship after relationship, I was my own worst enemy, thanks to my lack of self-esteem – I tolerated abusive situations because I didn't think I could do better. And I must've confused humility with humiliation, judging by how often I put with it. Connecting with my inner goddess changed all that, *completely*. Goddesses know that low self-esteem is a debilitating condition and refuse to give into it. Like an addiction, it gets worse with time; and we can't seem to walk away, even though we know its harmful effects. Why indulge in that? You're better off paying attention to what you do love about yourself versus what you disapprove of. You'll feel better and better about yourself, and realize that you're worth the life you hope for! And if you're still struggling with the humility issue, know that *humility is thinking of yourself less, not thinking less of yourself!*

9. Goddesses Know that Being Happy Outweighs Being Right: Most discussions heat up whenever someone tries to *prove* their point. If in doing so, an argument ensues, what difference does it make who's right at that point? Besides, your "opponent" will never see you as right in any case, certainly not when their emotions are running the show. Goddesses know that being happy outweighs being right, so they don't sweat the small stuff at a cost to their happiness. They know how to pick their battles and they aren't driven by the need to have the last word – now that's true power!

10. Goddesses Love Themselves to Bits: A goddess's mantra is not "Love thy neighbour as thyself", it's "Love thyself intensely and your neighbour will be happier living next to you." Either way, goddesses end up being happy, and everyone ends up loving them all the more, because they don't feel responsible for their happiness. Goddesses know that assuming the responsibility for your own happiness ensures that no one else has any control over you.

So if you want to feel powerful like a goddess, follow her "rules". Get back in the driver's seat and learn to "drive" your own life. "No" is not a bad word – it can be the most liberating word, in fact.

The easiest place to start is with small, attainable goals, such as, "I promise myself to say no to at least one thing that I don't want to do this week, and replace it with a yes to something I'd rather do, *for myself.*" In general, if there's something you want to do/buy for yourself, consider yourself worthy and find the budget to do it. If you don't love and spoil your inner goddess at least as diligently as you do your partner or child, then you're telling yourself that you're inferior to them. I'm not suggesting you become selfish; just take care of yourself *as well* as you do others. Women are often programmed to give to others but not to themselves, which can leave them feeling depleted and empty, but they're expected to keep going. It's critical that you replenish yourself and find your *joie de vie* without feeling bad about it. At times, that may even require you to put yourself first. That being the case, just remember what they say when you board a plane: "Secure your *own* oxygen mask before helping anyone else, including your kids".

What's even more powerful than all that is, enjoying your femininity on top of everything else! My grandmother used to say, "I wish women would give themselves the permission to be women, in all their sensual glory." I thought it was an odd statement coming out of a feminist's mouth. But when I talked to her about it, she said that being a woman is an honour, not an insult. She never got it when people felt insulted by being identified with that gender. She saw feminism as an uplifting, happy place, not something based in indignation.

The power to take charge and change your life is in your hands. So listen to your inner goddess and grab the reigns to your life. Feeling empowered is intoxicating. It'll make you just as giddy as getting in touch with your pussy power and your pussy.

Now take your sexy empowered self for a test drive, starting with flirting. Flirting is a great place to start, because it has no goal other than to feel good and make others feel good – i.e. enjoying yourselves in each other's presence. Unlike other activities that might be geared towards someone else, flirting is at least as much about you as it is about another.

As you read the next chapter, imagine yourself in various situations – or test them out for real. Then, focus on what happens inside you, how beautiful you feel, and perhaps how turned on you get, particularly when you pay attention to your pussy.

8: Flirting – The Lost Art

Have you ever wondered how some people can light up the room as soon as they walk in, draw people close like puppets on a string with a mere glance or smile, and demand attention from every corner? It's because their bodies advertise a feast of sensual delights, just dying to be savoured!

The one thing that these people have in common is, a mastery of body language and flirting skills.

But before we go any further, let's clarify the most common misconception – the difference between flirting and seducing. While seduction is about casting a line and catching a fish, flirting is about casting a net and catching *many* fish. In other words, flirting is about an attitude that allows us to enjoy *everybody*, not an activity geared toward seducing *somebody*.

By definition, to flirt means to court playfully, act amorously, or be coquettishly suggestive, all without serious intent. That in turn, eliminates fear of rejection, allows us to test out the waters innocuously, sweetens any deal, and charges up our lives with electricity that can convert the mundane to the magical. It's a simple yet effective way of being beguiling.

Furthermore, it's impossible to flirt without smiling, which in turn sends the message to our brain that we're happy. What other activity can do that for both parties involved?

To flirt, we need:

1. The Right Attitude: Keep it simple, fun, positive, interesting, and comfortable for everybody

2. The Right Vibe: Be the first one to establish eye contact, give a soft, closed-mouthed smile, tilt head to one side, and engage in the flirting triangle – glancing from left eye to right eye to chin, back to left eye; then repeat the flirting triangle with a slightly open-mouthed smile, with your head crooked to the other side

3. Understanding Body Language: Responsible for 93% of impression formation (words only count for 7%), according to Dr. Mehrabian

4. An Air of Ambiguity: You want them to think *maybe* you're interested, not definitely; even a wink can be crafted in a way that'll drive people crazy, since mystery can be a strong aphrodisiac

5. The Ability to Be Charming: Margaret Mitchell opens up *"Gone With The Wind"* with, "Scarlet O'Hara was not a beautiful woman, but men seldom realized it when caught by her charm" – and what charm she had, with guys swooning at her feet, hoping she'd pick them for a mere dance, while she flirtatiously enchanted them with her "innocent" charm

Beyond that, feel sexy on the inside by connecting with your inner goddess, be open to possibilities, and lay it on thick. It's a natural ability that we're born with – just watch babies smile, open up their body language, mimic our moves, and get bolder and bolder in the most flirtatious way imaginable, until we're completely hooked! FYI, when I logged on to hunt for pictures of people flirting, the majority of them consisted of babies who were unquestionably flirting with their naughty stares.

Sadly, society has trained us to suppress that natural skill that we were born with, if we have the slightest doubt that we might be wasting our time. Ironically, it's that very skill that can often get us what we want – so, time well spent – and it can be a delightful experience to boot.

The rules are pretty straightforward – here are my "10 commandments" for flirting.

10 Commandments of Flirting

1.   Keep it light and simple.

2.   Keep it safe. In other words, try to avoid the office or other places where it could create an awkward situation.

3.   Be unique in your approach.

4.   Feel your way out before trying anything too provocative.

5.   Do not misinterpret flirting for more than what it is – a non-consequential moment.

6.   Pick neutral topics to play with. Every situation consists of three things – you, the other person, and whatever brings you together (event, place, predicament, task). Pick the third neutral thing as your topic, especially when starting up a conversation with someone you don't know. For example, if you repeatedly run into someone in the morning coffee line up, tell them you feel like a change and would like them to recommend their favourite brand of coffee or pastry. Once you've broken the ice, you'll never pass each other again without at least a nod or a greeting, opening up new flirting venues.

7.   An ongoing flirtation must never be confused with a relationship. It is merely window shopping, if that, since we are rarely too picky about whom we flirt with.

8.   Learn to interpret body language and cues. Eye contact lasting longer than three seconds, resumed eye contact, head tilt, smile, grooming/stroking gestures on oneself, motion to catch your attention, are all signs of body flirting. If you find someone across the room trying out these moves on you, to the

point that they've piqued your interest, give them the opportunity to flirt more directly by moving away from your secure spot (especially if you're amongst your pack of friends).

Some people's entire body is a copulatory feast of flirtatious cues, accompanied by come-hither stares; learn to get good at it. Silly as it seems, practice in front of a mirror.

9.   Show your enthusiasm for the other person, slipping in innocuous little hints about your interest, when appropriate, to test out the waters. Double entendre and innuendos work in delicious ways. But save it for a social setting, not work, especially when there's a hierarchy between you and the other person.

10.   Above all, learn to have fun with it, without taking it too seriously. You'll be amazed at the liberties you can take. A girl I coached took it to an extreme, since she wasn't too worried about the consequences. One day, she caught a guy watching her in the subway, playing that ohmigosh-you-caught-me-staring-so-I'd-better-look-away-and-pretend-that-I-wasn't-staring game. She was really attracted to the guy, so when he started to get off the subway, without as much as a hello, she followed him out. Then, she tapped him on the shoulder and asked if he was looking at her. Embarrassed, he denied it. Boldly, she asked, "Why not, am I not pretty enough for you to stare at?" To which he responded "of course". She then asked, "Pretty enough to buy me a coffee, to make up for not giving me the time of the day when you should've?" And the rest as they say is their history.

When you do flirt, you may easily include compliments. But remember, always pick the third neutral thing. If you want to get more provocative, re-word the compliment to assign some form of credit to the complimented individual. For example, "You make that jacket look so hot" works much better than "Nice jacket" or "You look absolutely fabulous in that jacket".

While sticking to the non-threatening, neutral topic (clothing), the first example makes the individual the subject (versus the object) of the sentence, by attributing credit to them personally.

If you want to be very obvious in your attempt, without making the other person feel uncomfortable in any way, a casual approach is generally the best. Most people appreciate being the object of your attention. But you'll get a lot more out of flirting if you're a touch away from being too obvious. Remember, the idea is to let the other person think that *maybe* you're interested, not definitely. The "maybe" will work to your advantage, because their curiosity will make them work at finding out for sure.

To become a good flirt, you need to chant a mantra in your head – "I like myself. I'll try to like all other people, without exception, and bite my tongue on negative comments." This will allow you to become a fun people-loving person.

As discussed previously, flirting is not limited to people you already know. It can help you meet new people in fact. Here are a few helpful hints for that:

Flirting Tips to Meet People

1.   Sometimes a cliché can work if you decorate it with a ton of humour, laced with a flirtatious tone. For example, you may walk up to a person from behind, and say, "I'm sorry, but I thought you were someone else. ... Gosh, that sounds like a line, doesn't it?" But whatever you do, stay away from anything too personal as well as corny clichés, particularly if they're not too funny.

2.   Other times, you may be better off using the tried and tested method of offering the host/hostess your help in circulating food (unless they have catering staff). This will allow you to go to those who're not coming to you, with a legitimate excuse at that. When you arrive at your target, say, "I

love to offer my services to the host/hostess in passing things around at parties, since it gives me a chance to meet everybody. So, who might you be?" accompanied by your most flirtatious smile.

3.   At a bar, slip into the chair beside your prospect. Grab a napkin and start playing tic tac toe with them. Then, as you get going, slip in, "By the way, I'm ...." Or, if you're brave enough, "If we're going to be exchanging all these "x"s and "o"s (flirtatiously implying kisses and hugs), perhaps an introduction is in order?"

4.   Once you're speaking to a possible prospect, if someone tries to hone in on your territory, make your intention clear at the outset. Flirtatiously touch the person you're talking to on the arm, and say, "I can see that I'm going to have some stiff competition for your attention." Then quickly look the newcomer straight in the eye and say, "Can't say I blame you." This is harmless enough, but immediately makes your target feel attractive and the intruder feel like they're interrupting. People rarely find that comfortable and will want to move on. A two second gap of silence in this situation can feel like two hours, and make the intruder feel like they've interrupted something. Don't sweat it, they *have*! But whatever you do, don't be mean about it.

A goddess is *never* mean and knows when to move on. Even if things are going great, she leaves on a high note, so the other person is left craving more.

It's all about how we serve ourselves up – from facial expressions, to tone, to body language. The ideal tone is reached when you make sure that you have the most delish thoughts in your head. Try out the following exercise to get a feel for it.

Say "How would you like an ice cream?" three times, paying special attention to how significantly your tone and body language change, depending upon who you're offering it to.

The three people are:

1. A child

2. The last person you'd ever want to date

3. The person you'd most want to sleep with – the one that gets your pussy squirming

Notice the difference? Try out the last tone with someone you're *really* interested in at the next social gathering. But be playful about it; remember, no serious intention.

Good flirts keep it simple, light, and spontaneous. They end up attracting people in droves, by making them feel good about themselves, without any ulterior motives – they *genuinely* love people; it's not a manipulation tactic. You can spot them from a mile away, since they're the ones having the most fun, even when Mother Nature didn't necessarily give them the greatest assets. Often, the only thing they have going for themselves is, being open to possibilities.

And endless possibilities they have, everywhere they turn, because everyone wants to help them out, since they're on a first name bases with even the most casual of contacts. I know I've been helped out personally by many an individual, in many a situation, where they've gone to extremes for me, just because I always make a point of having fun with people, never willing to let it go at a simple "hello". And if I can make them feel good about something, all the better! But it always comes from the core of my heart, and in some cases the goddess demands it from me.

Body Language

"The eyes of men converse as much as their tongues, with the advantage that the ocular dialect needs no dictionary, but is understood the world over."

~ Ralph Waldo Emerson

Body language is the purest form of communication, since it's honest, free of pretentious words, universal, and deliciously subliminal. But a single gesture must never be given too much weight, since it's like a single sentence, which could mean any number of things, depending upon the context. Gesture clusters, on the other hand, can complete the picture in a remarkable way.

For example, if *all* clues point to open body language, the person is open to getting to know you better. If a person is full of life, having a great time *and* looking your way to include you, they're saying, "For a good time, join me."

Other examples of flirtatious gestures that can be clustered together, include the following:

1. Flirtatious glances

2. Gaze holding

3. Head-cocking

4. Rolling of the pelvis

5. In women, crossed legs that slightly expose the thigh

6. Placing a hand on the hip

7. Exposing the wrist or palm

8. Protruding breasts or derriere

9. Preening – particularly on an open thigh or wrist

Even if you're not entirely sure of what's going on, or how to pull it off, flirting is such a harmless activity that you can venture out without too much worry. A goddess loves the act so much that she throws herself into it without being too concerned about how she'll be received. Of course, there's a time and a place for everything. When looking for signals beyond the obvious ones we've already discussed, be aware of the following subtleties:

Reading Body Language in Others

1. A "come hither" look is an invitation to do just that and no more – come closer and strike up a conversation

2. A relaxed look shows that the person is comfortable with who they are and are likely to make you feel comfortable as well

3. Flared nostrils signal attraction

4. Personal space should reflect how emotionally close you want to get, not how desperately you want to touch; give an arm's length if the other person moves away, and touch only in the area between fingertips and elbows, when appropriate

5. Turned in shoes with toes pointing toward each other show that the person is getting nervous in a very good way; lay on the charm if you're truly interested

6. Exposed backhands – versus palms – signal that the person is claiming control of the conversation (perhaps fighting the "whipped" feeling); flirtation can go either way in that case

7. The direction that someone's upper body (chest and shoulders) points to is the biggest point of interest for them, independent of where their eyes are looking

8. Head cradled in the palm of a hand and shoulders pointing to the exit sign signals boredom; move on

9. Sexy thoughts dilate the pupils and subliminally suggest arousal

10. A smile combined with the eyes dropping down suggests interest combined with shyness

When you have someone's attention, stay focused on them, especially while they're talking, and break eye contact only when *you're* talking. You'll make them feel like they're the only point of interest for you – a very flattering feeling, which will mesmerize anyone. Many people who've watched me "working the room" – I wasn't even aware that I was doing that – observed that when I speak with someone, it's as if they're the only person in the room. It's because they truly have my undivided attention, just as I'd hope to have theirs.

Being focussed means avoiding *all* distractions, including checking your smart phone and other devices; even a quick glance can make a person feel neglected and break the rhythm.

The only thing you're allowed to think about is how delicious you are, and possibly how delicious the person is, whom you're flirting with. It'll change the tenor of your voice, just as deliciously as the ice cream example.

I can't tell you how many times that simple gesture has brought sheer joy and excitement to people. Various service personnel have shared how much they enjoy serving me – my florist, my butcher, my baker, and my candle-stick maker (just kidding with the last one). Some have gone so far as to say that it's the highlight of their day, because it leaves them smiling for the rest of the day. It's a meaningful experience because it's sincere, from my heart, since I love and enjoy people and always give them the benefit of the doubt when they're not at their best. You too are now ready to bring out the best in everybody, and conquer any situation delightfully. Just remember, you must practice, practice, practice, and you'll master the art like it's your second nature.Should you ever slip up, don't sweat it; keep in mind that the person you're trying to woo is probably too busy worrying about themselves to notice.

Finally, if there's still something that's holding you back, here are a few proven factoids that should boost your comfort level:

Flirting Mindset & Manners

1. More important than your body parts is the attitude who have toward them – this is more significant than you might realize, since flirting is a *total* body sport

2. Friendliness makes people appear a whole lot more attractive than they really are; what's flirtatiousness if not the ultimate in friendliness

3. People who rely on gut instinct make better decisions than people who rely on rationality and cold facts – learn to trust that *if in doubt, leave it out* instinct

4. People pair up with those who are roughly the same level of physical attractiveness, similar in age, intelligence, interests, education and social background

5. When someone's really drunk, that's their real personality; don't make excuses and flirt with them

6. We subconsciously inflate our opinions of others late at night, to make ourselves feel better about the dwindling options; buyer beware of late night flirting

7. Confidence and a great sense of humour will score you more dates than good looks

8. Simple opening lines allow you to simply slip into an interaction, so keep flirting simple

9. Body language experts believe that women should use more humour when flirting, men less

10. Always leave on a high and positive note

11. People who are intensely attentive mesmerize people better than anyone else

12. When flirting turns into something more serious, know that how soon you become sexually intimate is generally directly proportionate to how long the relationship will last

13. First impressions can be wrong, instincts rarely are; if your gut is telling you to stay away from someone, put your flirting on hold

14. Lust blindness can cause one to become more involved with the body than the mind, thereby pursuing relationships which aren't necessarily good for them – love is not blind, lust is

I have a friend – let's call her Jane – who swears by the above hints, since she's been living by those. She's fifty, doesn't have a cover-girl face or body, yet, she's the most sensual woman I know, who can date anyone she pleases. Whether she's in a relationship or flying solo, whenever she walks into a room, she has a huge presence – people stop and take notice. They're mesmerized by her sexual aura and will do anything she asks of them. It's her smile, the bounce in her walk, her flirtatious eyes, which make you wonder what she's thinking, and a tilt in her chin that says "I like you, anything's possible".

Time to go for it yourself – happy flirting! Just make sure you pay attention to *both* your brains – big and little – since they work in tandem, when your inner goddess is in charge.

I bet you're already feeling hot and sexy and being treated as such, meaning, you're ready to attract people in droves. You just have to learn how to own it and work it; Sophia Loren would be so proud, when you master the art!

9: Laws Of Attraction

According to Webster's dictionary: *to attract means to appeal to someone with a magical gravitational force, that entices and draws them near, providing pleasure and power.*

It's definitely something that a powerful, sexy, pussy-driven goddess would want, so she can rule the world. If you were here, I'm sure we'd be giving each other a pussy-likes-it high-five!

You've already figured out how to feel hot and sexy by now; it's time to dig a bit deeper to see how you can attract whomsoever you please, because there are some tried and tested laws of attraction that make it possible – just being attractive isn't enough in and of itself.

"How do I attract guys?" and "How do I attract girls?" seem to be the most frequently asked social questions, by singles wondering where all the eligible men and women are hiding? The irony: both genders seem to be looking for each other with equal fervour, yet coming up empty, even in cities where we rub shoulders with millions in the same boat, on a daily basis.

Being a matchmaker at heart, I decided to throw a singles' party, to address that very need for all my friends who were searching for that special someone, making it clear that it was a meet-and-mate-fest.

Alas, like most singles' events, despite a profusion of singles in proportionate ratios, most guests left alone, even though their questions/prayers had been answered, with tons of amazing possibilities staring them right in the face. Was I surprised? Not really, since even though they'd been brought together for the sole purpose of mingling, they lacked the know-how for making that first connection.

Right then, I decided to do extensive research to come up with a fool-proof method which would allow singles to stop asking the wrong questions and start connecting with the right persons – i.e., instead of asking where they can find eligible people, develop the skills to attract anyone, anytime, anyplace.

The possibilities are endless – you just have to learn how to attract them and make a connection!

First Impressions

When it comes to first impressions and initial reactions, which may well decide our futures in profound ways, we have but one chance to get it right.

What makes this especially challenging is, most of us assess, undress and best-guess long before a single word is spoken. In the first 30 seconds or less – average social attention span – we decide: friend or foe, flight or delight, opportunity or scrutiny, and make a yes or no decision before a person has had a chance to do their thing, even though we all agonize to perfect that "thing".

Naturally, the question which comes to mind is, "Can attention be held longer?" Absolutely! All you need to do is, create an intriguing presence, in terms of how you look, move, act, and interact with those around you.

Beyond that, your body language can also speak volumes on your behalf. Notice how some people can have an entire conversation from across the room, with their bodies speaking an orgy of languages, without them ever uttering as much as a single word? Why not you, especially since you've already learned how to work with body language?

Getting Started

First and foremost, you need to meet as many people as possible – if you don't meet them, how can you create opportunities?

So, accept as many invitations as you possibly can, sign up for hobbies/classes/meetups, join a gym, take transit every now and again, stand behind the most interesting person in a grocery line-up (you'll have their full attention in that moment), and so on. There's a feast of opportunities out there, no need to starve yourself.

I recall the movie *Sliding Doors* with Gwyneth Paltrow, where she misses the train by 1-2 seconds – had she not done that, her life would've been completely different.

My most significant relationship started out in such a moment – few seconds in either direction and my life would've been so different.

In any case, when those opportunities do pop up, you have to know how to navigate them flawlessly, so you can take a smile to a hello to the toughest part which comes after that – the first conversation. And by conversation I don't just mean verbal; I'm talking body language and tone as well – known to account for 93% of impression formation, according to a compelling study by Dr. Mehrabian.

So exactly how do you get that right? By learning how the other person's mind functions, so you may work with it to get the response you're looking for. Is this manipulation? Absolutely not! It's an important skill, if not the most useful one, which can be used to enhance opportunities wherever you go!

To meet someone, you need to:

1. Open up your body language – uncrossed arms & legs, open palms, and an unobstructed view to the heart area

2. Be the first to establish eye contact – possibly engage in a flirting triangle, with repeated gazes

3. Be the first to smile, once eye contact has been established – and hold it for 1-2 seconds instead of immediately looking away if "caught", because you *want* them to know that you're interested

4. Be the first to say hi/hello and possibly introduce yourself – stay clear of handshakes unless they're either warranted or the other person initiates them

5. Lean into the other party's direction and begin to synchronize your body language, voice tone/pitch, speech, etc.

Sound like a lot? Don't let it overwhelm you, since we're programmed from birth to use most of these elements to get what we want. Babies' body rhythms are synchronized with those of their mothers, and they have no problems getting what they want from others. They look you straight in the eye, smile at you, open up their arms (indicating open body language), and show their palms, all of which indicates that they're ready to connect. Next, they start to play the mimicking game with you for as long as you'll let them, to hold your attention.

It's an innate skill that you can practice at any time. And if you add in everything that you learned about flirting, you'll have no problem achieving that goal.

Furthermore, if your anticipated interaction involves a hot someone or the other, engage your pussy as well – she'll help you transmit the right signals, based in her animalistic instincts, and ultimately thank you for listening to her to achieve practically guaranteed results.

Beyond that, always have a positive attitude which will reflect in your body language and presentation – i.e. how we serve ourselves up. If you don't, no matter what you try to say, your body language will defy you.

That said, the initial interaction can still be quite confusing. Studies indicate that women send out more signals to pick up men than the other way around; though it doesn't always indicate "yes", just an interest in gathering up more information before making that decision. I guess that's another area where pussy power rules.

Many women just try to assess a guy's long-term potential, based on some list they have; others try to see how they'll fit into each others lives versus what looks good on paper. For them, it's about trusting their gut instinct – and of course their pussy instinct, when it comes to sexual chemistry.

Personally, I feel that if imagining being on a vacation with a guy – let alone spending your life with him – feels lacklustre compared to how much you'd enjoy yourself with your girlfriends, when you can be yourself, don't waste your attraction energy on him.

Keep an eye on him, but make sure the other eye is looking for someone more suitable – someone who fires you up in countless ways. My bestie has raised the bar on what being able to relax, laugh, be authentic, feel cared for, be encouraged, and just enjoying myself to the max looks like. If I can't feel those things with a partner, what's the point?

At the end of the day, why pick good on paper versus delicious, when you can have both? Otherwise, you'll always be searching for the unfulfilled side and end up in sticky situations; or worse – i.e., unfulfilled, and possibly unhappy. Neither your inner goddess nor your pussy want that for you!

Once your target passes the pussy instinct test, you can invest your energy in getting ready for the mating dance – yes, lay it on thick, while respecting the laws of attraction, so they work with you versus against you.

The Mating Dance

Assuming you've mastered the basic skills, let's put them in order, to attract that special someone who's worth your time and energy.

According to Dr. Perper, if you can manage the following steps of the mating dance, *in the right order*, you're guaranteed a repeat meeting. But if either party skips even one of these steps, however unintentionally, the chances of the interaction going any further will become next to nil.

5 Step Sequence to Guarantee An Initial Connection

1.   Non-Verbal Signals That Make One's Presence Known: a glance, smile, nod

2.   Verbal Contact: a hello, an intro, or a simple ice-breaker (nothing cheesy, witty, or complicated)

3.   Turning Toward Each Other: first heads, then shoulders, and gradually entire bodies must face each other

4.   Slightest Physical Contact: a reciprocated "accidental" touch (stiffening shows lack of interest), followed by eye contact perusing the body oh-so-subtly

5.   Synchronization: automatic body language mirroring (think babies) and voice tone synchronicity

Getting Someone to Like You

The key to getting someone to like you is, like yourself, like the other party, and show them that you like them *and* that you *are* like them – the first two are pretty self-explanatory, but the third one requires proper synchronization as well as speaking to their preferred modality, using the right sensory language.

Synchronization, as the word implies, means mimicking body language, via either mirroring or reflecting. It works well in assuring the person that you are like them, to create a certain comfort level. Whoever said that *imitation is the sincerest form of flattery* must've been referring to body language.

Preferred modality refers to the favoured sense that an individual uses to processes information, which in turn impacts the language style they employ.

According to the exact science of **Neuro-Linguistic-Programming** (NLP), there are three language styles, based on preferred sensory modalities: visual, auditory, and kinesthetic.

Visuals tend to visualize details and use graphic words to paint them just so. Auditories talk until they can get a sense of the whole story. Kinesthetics tend to be touchy feely and thrive on sensations, feelings and movements.

If you're trying to seduce someone or make them fall for you, you must speak their sensory language – it's akin to speaking to someone in their first language, or loving someone in their "love language".

So exactly how do we identify preferred modalities and sensory languages? Using the science of NLP, look for the following clues:

Visuals (55%)

- look obsessed / often sharp dressers

- fast talkers / often use hands to talk

- meticulous

- eyes look up to left when they recall, right when they construct (or lie)

- use expressions such as "see what I mean", "I see", "looks good" etc.

Auditories (15%)

- talk obsessed / often good communicators

- talk with average speed

- dress average

- eyes move from side to side (between ears), left when recalling, right when constructing (lying)

- use expressions such as "I hear ya", "in a manner of speaking", "I don't like the tone we're setting" etc.

Kinesthetics (30%)

- comfort obsessed

- comfy dressers, usually not too concerned with looks

- guys often have facial hair

- really fit or really slobby, depending upon whether they enjoy the physicality of exercise or the comfort of the couch

- touch and gesture a lot, and often pace – very entertaining to watch

- talk slowly and express details

- eyes move down to heart when talking, left for recall, right for constructing (lying)

- use expressions such as "she crawls under my skin", "he rubs me the wrong way", "I feel something's wrong" etc.

Once you know a person's favourite modality, you can speak to it. Speaking with someone using the right sensory modality is the difference between speaking to them in their first language versus second language. So if you're trying to engage, entice, or seduce someone, you have to use whatever they're most comfortable with, independent of your own preference.

Dale Carnegie's stated, "If you go fishing, although you may like strawberries, you put a worm at the end of the hook, because the fish likes worms."

If you follow these principles, with your amour in mind, you'll have no trouble attracting others.

But if you ignore the laws of attraction, you'll have trouble connecting, independent of how attractive you are – that's just window dressing, you need to follow up with tried and tested ways to keep them interested once they enter your space.

In general, laws of attraction – in any given area – stipulate that we attract what we focus on; so if you focus on the positive, the sexy, the fun, the pussy-friendly, you'll attract the same!

Now go for it – what are you waiting for?

10: No Time Like the Present

As a little kid, I was always curious about everything, including the meaning behind fairy tales and fables – small wonder I didn't buy into the Prince Charming stuff.

What really intrigued me was the fable of Aladdin and his magic lamp. I wondered why it was so dusty and why the genie had been locked up for so long, when he could make wishes come true?

The only answer, which made sense was, we make our wishes come true when we're good and ready. The magic and the resources stay hidden somewhere until then – forgotten, gathering up dust. And so it is with many individuals and their dreams.

When I ask people about their dreams, most say that they can't remember them. And they're so lost that they've given up on even finding them. It's generally because life has taken over, or they've been so busy servicing other people's dreams that they've forgotten their own.

I then ask them what they were doing as kids when mom called out to them for dinner – that one thing that they had a hard time tearing themselves away from? Were they playing outside, were they hanging out with friends, were they reading, were they playing a musical instrument, were they playing a game, were they playing house, were they pretending to be in a movie like my cousin and I used to? Suddenly their faces light up and they become really animated as they start to share their stories.

From there, we get into what they loved about the particular activity, and their heart's desires surface. At that point, I want them to expand their minds to envision possibilities, without limitations; so I ask them, if money, time, status, training, family, and their lifestyle weren't an issue, what would they do?

I can't tell you the joy I experience in that moment, as they connect the dots and light up. I know then that they're ready to dust down their lamp and make their wishes come true.

For a woman who's ready to manifest herself as her authentic self, this is the time to let that inner goddess out of hiding, so she'll help her become who she's always wanted to be. And her pussy will provide the fuel to kick her sensuality into full gear, to ensure that it's one hellova fun ride getting there! I want nothing short of that for you, because trust me, it's the best way to live your life!

The time to start is right now, in this moment. It isn't when your kids grow up, you lose weight, you save more money, you get married, you get that promotion or raise, your ailing parent passes on, your kids move out of the house, or anything else that's in the way. How are things going to be any different then?

I mean really? Will you have more time, a better cash flow, a healthier body? To me that's pretty ironic, since being a goddess means making life better on all counts, in the moment, not *waiting* for it to become better, so you can start enjoying it.

The journey can be at least as much fun, but you have to be willing to do the work and really get into it.

Let's begin, starting with a brief inventory of your desires and roadblocks. FYI, fear is the number one roadblock – and the flipside to need – so we'll be looking into that specifically.

Reconnecting With My Dreams

Answer the following questions as truthfully as you can; set aside your limitations for now.

1. What are my biggest hopes and dreams?

2. If I haven't fulfilled them yet, what's stood in the way?

3. What are my biggest fears?

4. Where do my fears come from – what beliefs, memories, discouragements do they tie into?

5. What makes me the happiest?

6. What makes me the most miserable?

7. What do I need to change about my life?

I now want you to think about the person you want to become – based on what makes you *happy*, what makes you *miserable*, and what you'd like to *change*.

Next, I want you to envision the divine creature you dreamed of becoming. Is that person living authentically, confident, happy with themselves, able to show off their positive traits unapologetically, and love and accept their negative traits without shame?

Once you can do that, it's time for you, your goddess, and your pussy to come up with a mission statement. Ideally, mission statements are a single sentence that allows us to stay focussed on our desires, what we want for ourselves, what fires us up, what makes us look forward to each day.

You're now ready to formally begin your work. To keep yourself focussed on what you envision for yourself, you'll need to make a Vision Board, so you don't lose sight of it.

Getting Ready for My Vision Board

Find pictures that represent or symbolize the experiences, feelings, sensuality, vitality, and possessions you want to attract. Have fun with the process. Use photographs, magazine cut-outs, pictures from the Internet – whatever inspires you. Be creative. Include not only pictures, but also anything that speaks to you, like words or sayings.

Find a picture of yourself that was taken in a happy moment, for the center of your board. It should be surrounded by your affirmations, inspirational words, quotations, and delicious thoughts. Choose words and images that inspire you and make you feel good – don't forget your pussy's wishes.

Be very selective with what you put on your vision board. You must avoid anything that doesn't fire you up with strong emotions. Too much stuff makes for a cluttered or disorganized board, which can attract chaos into your life. So it's really critical that you only choose that which truly represents your purpose, your ideal future, and words that inspire positive and delicious thoughts in you. There is beauty in simplicity and clarity. Too many images and too much information will be too distracting.

6-Step Process for Making an Empowering Vision Board

1. Create a list of goals you'd like to achieve in the next year – you need to be able to visualize those clearly. So take the time to envision exactly what you want your ideal life to look like, and what you need to accomplish in the next 12 months to bring you closer to your goals.

2. Schedule a couple of hours to go through your collection of words and images, and select only those which speak to your heart in some meaningful way – i.e., those that immediately make you say, "Yes! That is what I want in my life!" They don't have to be physical objects or literal interpretations of what you want in your life. Instead, focus on how the images make you FEEL.

3. Make a collage out of your photos on your vision board. Glue, tack, or tape your pictures to the poster in an arrangement that is visually pleasing to you.

4. Add motivational "affirmation words" that represent how you want to FEEL.

5. Your vision of your ideal life shouldn't be focused on "stuff" so much as on how you want to FEEL – e.g., joyful, abundant, powerful, fearless, loved, strong, healthy, sensual, authentic, financially free, in control, confident, and so on. If you didn't find powerful words to post on your board, you can always write them down yourself, because they need to convey emotions precisely.

6. Take a few minutes, once or twice every single day, to contemplate your vision board. For this reason, it's really important that you place it somewhere where you can't help but see it.

The best time for visualization is first thing in the morning, and the last thing at night – two very powerful moments in programming your brain.

The thoughts and images that you begin each day with will help you generate a vibrational match for the future you desire. And the thoughts and images that are present in your mind in the last forty-five minutes before going to sleep will be the ones that will replay themselves repeatedly in your subconscious throughout the night.

It's a good idea to create a new vision board each year. As you continue to grow, evolve and expand, your dreams will follow suite. Your vision board can chronicle your dreams as well as your growth and achievements.

Next, you'll be taking the first step towards seeing your goals to fruition, particularly with respect to the order that you need to observe, to accomplish those goals.

My Goal Grid

Write down all the changes that you need to make to have the life you want – the life on your vision board. Beside each, enlist the steps you'll need to take, followed by the impact each decision will have on your life, the level of importance you assign to each, and the courage to pursue those steps.

Courage Index:

1 hoping / 2 wishing / 3 wanting / 4 intending / 5 at any cost

Ranking (level of importance):

1 minimum / 2 some / 3 average / 4 very / 5 critical

Goal	Steps to Take	Impact on Life	Rank	Courage Index
Eg: Better sex life	Eg: Journal what I want, why, organize thoughts, speak with partner	Eg: Happier healthier, better relationship, lack of resentment	Eg: 5	Eg: 3

Once you've completed the table, do an assessment. In the example above, of concern would be the fact that it's a critical decision (rank of 5), yet the courage to purse is only 3, which stands for "wanting", versus 5, which stands for "at any cost".

Once you work through your discrepancies, set **SMART** goals – i.e., **S**pecific, **M**easurable, **A**ttainable, **R**ealistic & **T**ime Sensitive. This will allow you to break everything down into smaller, more easily attainable (realistic) goals that have a timetable attached to them, to keep you moving, and to give you an opportunity to celebrate fulfilment at each stage. The last part is absolutely critical – your pussy will agree – because everything will only work if you're having fun and you stay at it. Doubly so if you start to act as if you're already there!

I knew a lady who used to come to a hair salon that I went to. We ran into each other every single month, since our appointments were in the same cycle. What really impressed me about her was, she not only had a vision for her life, she lived it.

She had the salon store a place setting of fine china, silverware and crystal for her. Since we were there for a good 3-4 hours, we had to have a lunch break somewhere in there. The restaurant next door had the most fabulous Mediterranean food. So she would order herself lunch from there, and generously tip the shampoo girl to pick up the food for her and place it on her fine china, and pour her Perrier into her crystal flute. She ate sumptuously and glamorously like a queen, not someone trying to ensure that her plastic fork doesn't puncture through a cheap Styrofoam box.

I generally ordered the same food, but it didn't look nearly as good; I certainly didn't, sitting slouched in my chair versus upright like I was dining at an emperor's table. Needless to say, I decided to do the same for myself. I'm pretty sure the salon wasn't crazy about storing those things for us, but when you give proper gratitude and gratuity, everyone's aboard.

Don't wait for others to do what you need to do for yourself. And never ever apologize for doing that which aligns with your dreams, desires, hopes, you feeling like a queen!

I hosted a call-in radio show – Intimate Moments with Rebecca – where people rang in to speak with me, from all over North America due to the huge bandwidth.

One night, a lady called in, right after her husband had passed away from a long battle with cancer. She hadn't even spoken to her family yet; I suppose she was waiting to find the courage to tell her children. When she shared what had just happened, we cried together and I asked her what she'd miss the most about him? She said, "Being his Princess, because that's how he always referred to me, and indeed how he treated me."

We played Bette Midler's song, *Wind Beneath my Wings*, and dedicated it to him, even though it wasn't a music show. I then encouraged her to buy a tiara whenever she felt up to it, and to wear it every time she wanted to feel like his princess.

She went the very next day, bought herself the most beautiful tiara she could find, and wore it to his funeral. She didn't care what anyone thought of her dressing like a princess, versus wearing all black, with a black hat and veil. It was her way of honoring his memory and honoring herself as the princess that she was.

Go buy yourself a tiara, a boa, sexy clothing, power suit, toys for you pussy, flowers for your home, candles for your bathtub, and whatever else tickles your fancy, and revel in decadence; because moving forward, that's what your life is gonna look like. You get to choose how you want to live it, and how you want to feel because of it!

The time to start is right now, in this very moment. Put down the book for a moment, and pause to envision your new life. Make notes, journal as you go along, and find a friend to be your cheerleader.

Agree that you'll both start each conversation with bragging about something. And if either one of you slips into negative self talk, they'll have to counteract that with five points to brag about.

You can also act like each others 12 step sponsor, so if you're headed into trouble, you can call each other up before slipping too close to the ledge, or taking steps backwards.

This can also work as a solo exercise. Every time you are self-critical, you have to come up with three reasons to praise yourself, ideally connected to whatever you're critical of. It's all about checks and balances – and showing up on your behalf.

I end my email with:

It's your life, make it exceptional! ~ It's a part of my email signature to help people remember this simple truth. And apparently, it has impacted many individuals. So set that intention for yourself – there's tremendous power in that!

The second half of the book is dedicated to relationships, whether you are in one, you want one, or you choose to have one in the future. But it always has to start with you being your very best, so you can carry that into your relationships.

If you choose not to be in a relationship, that's fine as well. You may just skip the next section altogether, or pick up bits and pieces that apply to all relationships, not just romantic ones.

PART B

CONNECTING SENSUALLY WITH MY LOVERS

11: Relationships – The Final Frontier

If you've chosen to fly solo, play the field, try out a different lifestyle, I love you and applaud you for honoring your authenticity.

But since we can't avoid relationships altogether, I hope this section will be beneficial to you all the same, even though a lot of the stuff is geared towards navigating through coupleships. I felt compelled to write it, because relationships can be at the crux of how we experience life, but there's not much instruction on enjoying them in healthy ways, just lots of self-help books for fixing what's broken, after the fact.

Is your relationship like a Rubik's cube, that gets more and more distorted with each twist; or is it like a kaleidoscope that offers beautiful new possibilities at every turn? The former gets more and more complicated the harder we try to force it to go a certain way; the latter just unfolds seamlessly, always open to new horizons and possibilities.

So why exactly do some couples get stuck in the former versus embracing the latter? Because each party gets caught up in their own feelings, and then they struggle with their need to belong.

According to Maslow's Pyramid, the need to belong, to be accepted, and to be intimate are placed right alongside the need for food, shelter and safety, because they're all primal needs, essential for our survival and well-being. Hence the need for belonging is one of the greatest motivators of human behaviour; in intimate relationships, it's the need for acceptance by a partner.

As such, if one's partner doesn't accept them, they can end up hiding who they really are and suppressing their desires, which eventually turns into resentment – the reason that your inner goddess will never condone you suppressing any parts of yourself.

What makes the whole process even more complicated is, our fear of rejection, which ties into the two biggest relationship fears that people have: the fear of losing the other person, and the fear of losing the self to hold onto the other person.

Furthermore, since women are generally the emotional gatekeepers, they tend to accommodate everybody else, at a cost to themselves. So the fear of losing the self is always running in the background, like a computer program, but they try to ignore it.

It's high time that you start paying attention to it, because that program is goddess software, telling you to love without losing yourself. Not only will you respect yourself more, so will your partner.

Every day, I end up seeing at least a couple of women doing individual therapy, who've given their heart and soul to their partners – and families – and lost themselves in the process.

They're upset that they did so much for their partner, but they were still neglected and unappreciated, and now they're done!

I ask them if they ever attempted to fix it, before getting to this stage, and they invariably say no.

When I ask them why not, their answers range anywhere from "I didn't want to upset him," to "I don't think it would've mattered," (without actually putting it to a test), to "If I do things my way, he'll resent me; if I do things his way, I'll resent him. So I'd rather resent him than the other way around." None of these make sense to me.

In couples therapy, a common theme is sexual dissatisfaction. Interestingly, while most women go over the top taking care of everything else, sex gets put on the back burner – possibly because they're too tried after taking care of everything else. The sad part is, many of these women do want sex, lots of it, but they don't prioritize it.

If any of this resonates, stop right now! Put the book aside, connect with your inner goddess, and have a conversation with your pussy. Ask her if she's happy with the current arrangements? If not, have her go to town before doing anything else. I'm assuming you've already read Part A, so you are well-versed in how to do that, full on, with toe curling extended orgasms, even though that should never be the ultimate goal.

Going back to relationships, most men will trade a dirty house for a dirty girl any day – trust me, I've heard it enough times – meaning, we need to spend more time enjoying sex than grinding through chores. It'll also make for a more pussy-attuned, goddess-approved existence, which is a lot more fun, by far, independent of what guys may prefer.

Outside of that, here are some relationship rules that'll take care of the other stuff.

10 Commandments for Healthy Relationships

1.	Some relationships click, others tick like a time bomb – the difference lies in whether or not you allow your negative thoughts to overwhelm your positive ones, both with respect to your situation as well as your partner. So no analysis paralysis that keeps you living in *past* hurts or *future* fears – deal with them and then commit to enjoying the *present*, since it's a gift after all.

2.   Nurturing and expressing your fondness and admiration for each other is one of the best ways you can divorce-proof your relationship. No matter what stage your relationship is at, it'll help you sustain that intimate bond, whereas criticism will only destroy it. According to Dr. John Gottman, the ideal ratio of praise to criticism is 5 to 1 – most of us aren't even halfway there.

3.   Contrary to popular belief, compassion is the most important attachment emotion, not love, since it binds us together through time of need, in meaningful ways. So be sure to be there for each other; and when you can't be a part of the solution, show support and ensure that you don't become a part of the problem.

4.   There is no absolute reality in any situation, just two subjective realities, influenced by three long histories – yours, your partner's, your relationship's. So listen to understand your partner and be influenced by them, versus trying to bend them to your will – they'll be happier and you'll become irresistible. If things get out of hand anyway, do the first thing they teach you in driving class – put on the brakes, to avoid a disaster.

5.   When you start to feel angry, identify what's really making you angry, follow it to its source, and try to understand what it's telling you, since anger is rarely about the final straw; it's generally a secondary emotion to whatever triggers it. And if it starts to hijack your mind, body or soul – your heart starts racing, you feel flushed, you get a knot in your stomach – know that there is no possible way of being rational at that time. Ask for a break, and wait for that chemical rush to die down, so your anger doesn't italicize everything! But a break isn't a get out of jail free card; you'll need to have a discussion at some point, just not when you're experiencing those physical sensations, meant to prepare you for a fight or flight.

6.   While communication is important to a relationship, the *way* you communicate is even more important. Words can hurt, destroy, kill relationships, but can't be taken back. So when you "talk", think connection, not communication, making a conscious effort to take care of each-others' needs.

7.   When you have a difference of opinion, use power tools that repair, instead of weapons that kill. The four deadliest weapons are: criticism, defensiveness, stonewalling, and contempt – identified by Dr. John Gottman as the Four Horsemen of the Apocalypse.

8.   When you're not sure how to act in a given situation, think of what's best for the relationship, not either party – it'll keep both selfishness as well as resentment at bay.

9.   If you need something, ask for it, versus complaining about what you're not getting. And when your partner asks you for something – for instance, more time with you – respond to their longing, versus feeling criticized and reacting to it. It's important to find out what a request symbolizes, instead of dismissing it as unreasonable; so try to understand where your partner is coming from, versus protesting to hold your own ground.

10.   Love is the irresistible desire to be desired irresistibly. Never lose sight of that. Ask yourself at the end of each day what nice things you did for your partner and what you could've done differently. In other words, why would they wanna stay with you; or for that matter, would you wanna be married to someone like yourself?

I grew up in a household where I had a front row seat to one of the healthiest relationships I've ever seen, between my mom and dad, who were married for nearly sixty years, until he passed away. Not only were they in love until the very end, they were also crazy about each other.

You could see them catch each other's eye across the room, with that new love smile and mischief in their eyes. You could see him give her a squeeze when he thought no one was watching.

And then there were the mood lights that he kept buying for their bedroom. But the most significant moment that's forever branded in my brain – almost like it was yesterday – took place just a few days before he passed.

He'd been in the hospital for several days – unshaved, unkept, cheeks dented because he had become gaunt, and he was resisting baby food since he loved to eat well his entire life. So here he was, a man who'd taken a great deal of pride in always being impeccably put together, looking his worst, but my mom looked at him like he was an exquisite work of art.

And then it happened – a mid-twenties, stunning nurse came into the room and said, "How are we doing, Sweetheart?" Wouldn't you know it, my mom became very jealous because she thought this woman was trying to pick him up. I told her that she had nothing to worry about, expecting her to notice the obvious. But she held her ground and shared what was *her* obvious truth – *he was the most gorgeous and amazing man in the world, so any woman in her right mind would make a play for him.* It blew my mind with how she saw him.

Their secret: patience, love, lust, and always being on the same side, because it would break their heart to see the other party in pain. I'm sure they made mistakes and had issues like all couples do, but it's how they handled those and how quickly they forgave each other to get back on track that made all the difference. They couldn't stand to be mad at each other!

A goddess knows that in a coupleship if one party wins, both parties win; but if one party loses, both parties lose. She never gets caught up in making unnecessary points, when she'd rather spend her time making love – i.e. she always believes in being happy versus being right. Her pussy concurs, meaning, both of her heads are focused on the same goal – her happiness – so they help her make that choice.

That said, even if your pussy is in pussy heaven, having a time of her life, if the relationship feels toxic, you gotta walk, girl. Trust me, your pussy is smart and will understand – mine actually goes on strike if I'm unhappy with my partner, to keep me on track!

And if you have to engage in some *ménage à moi* to take care of yourself while flying solo, your pussy won't mind at all. She'll see it as being indulged by the person who loves her the most, *exactly* the way she likes it, so you'll be shouting out your own name. It may not involve crazy gymnastics or chandeliers, but it'll be warm, fuzzy, comfortable and familiar, like the inside of an UGG® boot, or a cozy blanket, but with a more spectacular crescendo.

At the end of the day, a relationship/partner should add something awesome to your life, not be a means to completing it, because that implies that you aren't whole without it, which is a recipe for disaster.

It's better to fly solo than to end up in a relationship that outright sucks. Hopefully that'll cure your fear of: #WhatIfIEndUpAlone and help you see it as: #StupidShitWeMakeUpToKeepOurselvesInBadRelationships.

In that spirit, let's look at breaking unhealthy relationship patterns next.

12: Breaking Unhealthy Relationship Patterns

Have you ever found yourself in one unhealthy relationship after another? Is the real you buried so deep beneath the facades you must maintain in order to feel loved, that you don't even know who you are anymore?

Well, that stops right now – neither your inner goddess nor your pussy are going to have any of it. It's time to take another look at the kind of men you gravitate toward, and see if they pass the "health test". Herewith a list of ten habits that separate healthy men from unhealthy ones.

10 Commandments for Healthy Men

1.   Healthy men have healthy relationships with their mothers. They adore them, respect them, are regularly in touch with them, but they've cut the umbilicus, so they aren't enmeshed. Beyond that, they have a huge fan-base amongst friends, relatives, colleagues and acquaintances – everyone loves them, because they're easy to get along with and know how to navigate relationships.

2.   Healthy men do not come undone at the slightest provocation. How a man handles aggravating driving conditions, minor disappointments and uncooperative electronics is how he'll handle you, when you're not your perfect self. Healthy men are responsive versus reactive – you'll rarely find them in a bad mood for no good reason!

3. Healthy men know what makes them happy and they cherish it – i.e., they neither take it for granted, nor do they jeopardize it. If he hasn't figured out how to be happy by now, he never will; and no matter what you do, it won't make a difference, other than frustrating the heck out of you.

4. Healthy men work on bettering themselves throughout their entire lives. They're successful in many areas, their efforts show constant growth, new opportunities, new possessions, and progression versus regression. An unhealthy man can keep very busy with things that amount to nothing significant.

5. Healthy men bring out the best in you. If you're having a bad day, they'll remind you of how great you are – their positive, adoring view of you will remain unchanged. Unhealthy men forget all the good in you the minute you do/say something wrong – their perception of you changes based on the circumstances, not your overall character.

6. Healthy men will never make you feel bad about yourself, even when you're in the middle of an argument. They view you as an ally, not the opposition, and know the value of nice begetting nice. They actively make choices that make for a happy relationship. Unhealthy men don't care about how you really feel when the chips are down, draw erroneous conclusions without listening to you, take everything personally, and bring out the big weapons to attack, when all they need is a little tool to fix. Problems are thereby rarely resolved. At best, they'll give you lip service instead of real change; at worst, they'll just negate/dismiss your feelings.

7. Healthy men appreciate what you do for them – however big or small. They never minimize your contributions, make you feel like it's never enough, or forget to reassure you of how important you are and all the good you bring into their lives. An unhealthy man has a hard time thanking you or apologizing to you – he's afraid that you'll keep track.

Everything needs to be on his terms anyways, with you only mattering in so far as how you fit into his life, not how he fits into yours.

8.   Healthy men are consistent, whether they're with you, at work, talking to a stranger, or at a party. An unhealthy man is a chameleon – he changes to meet his own needs. When he's drunk, his true colors show, since his defenses are down; observe how he behaves then, because that's the man you'll be living with once he gets comfortable with you, since that's who he is at his very core.

9.   Healthy men are unselfish. They respect your needs and support your dreams and commitments, even if it puts them out. Compromise is not a dirty word with them – they see it as combining assets and building something wonderful together. They know that relationships are like bank accounts – you can only take out what you put in, with interest.

10.   Healthy men are trustworthy and treat you in ways that you're never left wondering if he's the right guy, where he might be, what he's up to, how does he really feel about you and other important things. They include you in their lives – even when they're doing their own thing, you need never worry about it. Unhealthy men make you wonder about your place in their world.

Beyond all of that, here's my list of additional guy facts, compiled from some very wise women, who have their pick of men, since they line up to date them. These are the women who never have to worry about landing a guy, or getting their pussy serviced the way *they* want!

There are 30 facts for you to master over the next thirty days. Spend an entire day contemplating each fact, until it sinks in.

30 Crucial Guy Facts that Women Need To Know

1.   Guys don't mind messing up a friendship if it could lead to great sex; don't buy it if he tells you otherwise. If he was interested, he would've already tried to mess around with you by now.

2.   Should you ask a guy out? If he was truly interested, he would've already asked you out, or at least dropped some major hints.

3.   Why don't guys call when they say they will? Most guys hate confrontation (think what happens when you want to "talk") and will say whatever it takes to maintain the status quo when ending a conversation/date. Why get into it when you don't have to? Doubly so with someone you don't intend to see again! So next time a guy says he'll call, don't wait for it; if he really wants to see you again, he's likelier to say, "When can I see you again?"

4.   Should you call him? If a guy hasn't bothered to extend the courtesy of a phone call to you, why would you wanna chase that down? ... No, he didn't lose your number!

5.   For most people sex is one of the greatest joys in a relationship. If your guy is keeping you from enjoying it, dump him, sell the damn bling he gave you, and invest it in something else that gives you joy. If you have money left over, buy your pussy a little toy. And while you're at it, buy one for your bestie as well – you know, the one with the loser boyfriend that she's been clutching onto, just because he lubes her up with pussy juice (for his own sake).

All this applies doubly so, if he shames you for your sexual desires; get out fast in that case. World famous cartoonist, Alison Bechdel, known for her long-running comic strip, *Dykes to Watch Out For*, couldn't have put it better, in saying, "... a lifetime spent hiding one's erotic truth could have a cumulative renunciatory effect. Sexual shame is in itself a kind of death."

6.   Him slipping his penis into someone else doesn't just happen – it's well executed in the first degree – so no get-out-of-someone-else's-vagina-free cards!

7.   After a break-up, still having feelings for him doesn't in any way translate into still having sex with him – no matter what he says!

8.   Doesn't matter why he left: the point is he left. Quit beating yourself up already by pushing for a reason – do you really want to know why he doesn't feel like seeing you ever again? Ditto for trying to figure it out by yourself. Trust me, nothing you come up with will make you feel okay, and you won't know for sure anyways. This also applies to trying to figure out why a guy cheated on you.

9.   If the world just revolves around him, with every rotation you'll get more and more screwed – and not in a good way. Find someone who spends as much time thinking/worrying about you as you do him.

10.   Bad boys are generally bad for you – don't expect one to suddenly turn into Mr. Right. But as far as Mr. Right-Now goes, look no further.

11.   Whatever he says, it doesn't count if he just says it after/during/while-hoping-for sex, or when he's high.

12.   Cutting him off isn't about making him miss you – it's about you discovering you're fine without him.

13.   If he asks you to lose 20 pounds, lose him instead. It'll be like losing everything he weighs plus how he weighs you down, all at once – will make for an interesting before/after shot, with you looking more confident than ever!

14.   When he makes an excuse for why he can't see you, it may be a polite rejection; but when *you* make an excuse for him not being able to see you, that's just stupidity – or self-torture, if you keep waiting for things to change. I'd rather you buy heels that hurt, or be hog-tied for fun, versus putting yourself through that.

15.   If you've been dating for five or more years sans any form of commitment – exclusivity, engagement, moving in together, etc. – chances are that it'll never happen. If you want it, don't wait for it; get it from someone else. In general, if there's no progression in a relationship, or he holds all the cards, he's just stringing you along. Even the best sex or lifestyle isn't worth it – this is one time that you might have to ask your pussy to simmer down, or give her something better to feast on.

16.   Grovelling like a pathetic, desperate fool never made any guy change his mind about a woman. Besides, how attractive is that? It certainly won't endear you to him.

17.   If you really love someone you want to make them happy, not sad. Take a hint from your gut feeling – yes, that feeling sometimes lives in the pussy.

18.   Nothing can keep a guy away from someone he truly digs – that includes busyness and fear of intimacy. Again, don't make excuses for him, or buy into his.

19.   How can you feel worthy of love if someone is going out of their way to make you feel unworthy?

20.   Life is tough enough; you don't need someone who makes it tougher – unless of course you're a masochist, in which case you might as well buy a doggie collar so your friends can stop worrying.

21.   Think of yourself as the rule, not the exception. And no, you're not going to be the one who'll make him change his mind; if he wanted that, he would've figured it out for himself.

22.   "Better than nothing" is never a good enough reason to stay – there's always something better, even flying solo, pursuing your dreams and checking out what else is out there. Make a pact with your friends that they commit you if you commit to someone awful, because that makes you certifiably insane.

23.   If he can't be bothered to tell you what's going on, according to him nothing special is going on – between the two of you that is.

24.   Why do men love bitches? Because they won't settle for anything less than what serves them – remember she's a Babe In Total Control of Herself?

25.   If he's not into monogamy and you are, what kind of cruel experiment are you sticking around for?

26.   If the guy you dig would rather shop and cook with you than try to get you naked, he's not a keeper – he's just not into you. Find someone who is.

27.   If he's just not into you, don't take it personally; move on to someone who digs you.

28.   If he criticizes your pussy in any way, kick him to the curb. No one gets to micromanage her, including yourself – she's a smart cookie, so work *with* her instead of *against* her.

29.   If the only time he does nice things for you is because there's some benefit in it for him, and never when there's nothing in it for him, he's in the relationship for himself, not you. So quit judging how wonderful he is based on just those moments.

30.   How he behaves is who he is; what he says is who he wants you to *think* he is, which is the same as manipulation – the worst form of lying.

I could go on, but you get the drill – it's about mutual respect, knowing your self-worth, and not settling for anything less. It's a truly empowering feeling!

Beyond all that, I'd be remiss if I didn't address co-dependence in this chapter, since far too many women end up in co-dependent relationships (and some men as well). So let's talk about that next.

Co-dependence

By definition, co-dependency means making the relationship more important than yourself. It can be one-sided, because one party is trying to make the relationship work, with someone who may have checked out.

When the less invested party behaves badly, the co-dependent party tries to put up with them, or fix the situation. It could be the result of them feeling that they're not good enough, so they have no choice but to put up with it; or because that dynamic makes them feel like they're the better person, so it helps their poor sense of self; and possibly makes them feel that they'll eventually be recognized and/or rewarded for their hard work, because they rely on the other party to feel good about themselves.

Co-dependency symptoms are common in (but not limited to) people who grew up in dysfunctional homes. They get used to pain, conflict, and dealing with emotionally disengaged individuals, so they accept those things from their partners, whereas others may not. But accepting doesn't mean that they hurt any less; or for that matter, they aren't triggered by them.

So, how do you know if *you're* in a co-dependent situation? Ask yourself the following three questions:

1.   Is this relationship more important to me than I am?

2.   Am I paying a high price for being with this person?

3.   Am I the only one putting energy into this relationship and doing all the heavy lifting?

To check if you have a tendency towards co-dependent relationships in general, see if you display one or more of the following patterns:

•   People pleasing – giving too much in relationships

•   Avoiding conflict

•   Relying on others for defining self-worth

•   Having poor boundaries

•   Ignoring red flags – at one point I was like a bull; I'd see a red flag and charge for it

Interestingly, even smart, successful, self-reliant individuals can end up in co-dependent situations. I've worked with many people who were at the top of their game professionally, but when it came to their relationships, all that self-assuredness went out the window.

If any of this resonates, it's important for one to do a mental inventory, to determine if they believe that love is supposed to be painful, because of what they saw growing up. That being the case, people can self-sabotage their chances of having a healthy relationship, where they can get their needs met, versus confusing drama and intensity with intimacy. Unless one owns that part and works on it, they're just as responsible for unhealthy relationship patterns as the partner they blame.

That said, even those who repeatedly end up in the latter scenario may eventually get to the point where they feel they've had enough – and that can be the moment which nudges them towards healthy change. The willingness to leave is often what sets things straight at that point. But it has to be a genuine effort to want better for oneself, not a game where one hopes they'll make the other person miss them – or teach them a lesson, for that matter – because it's still about the other party in that case, which is at the crux of co-dependence.

As a sidebar, co-dependent individuals are often drawn to troubled, distant, or moody people, and can't tear themselves away from them – despite being treated badly by them – but they can dismiss "nice" candidates as "boring". Eventually, their unhealthy situation makes them spiral down, because nothing erodes self-esteem quicker than an unhealthy relationship. The good news: co-dependent individuals *can* heal, reclaim their lives, and end up in healthy relationships, if they:

•   Visualize themselves in loving relationships which meet their needs – mindfully experience what that looks like, using all five senses. This is especially great when done at bed-time, when the subconscious mind is ready to be reprogrammed (as our sleep takes our mind into the beta-theta zone).

•   Challenge their beliefs and self-defeating thoughts about their self-worth, every time they pop up in their head – Cognitive Behavior Therapy can really help with that.

• Become kind and compassionate towards themselves. It's healthy to accept help when needed – seeing a therapist could be a game-changer.

• Disallow their fear of rejection to stop them from achieving loving, intimate relationships. Being drawn to broken people to minimize rejection is nothing more than faulty, self-defeating thinking; and FEAR is no more than False Expectations Appearing Real!

For more information on addressing co-dependence, I highly recommend Melody Beattie's book, *Co-dependent No More* (Hazelden Publishers, 1986).

Since a lot of what we've covered ties into knowing your self-worth, allow me to end this section by sharing a story with you.

An elderly man was dying. He called out to his son, showed him a 200-year-old watch, and said, "This is your grandfather's watch – I'd like to give it to you. But before I do, I want you to go to the watch shop and ask what they'll give you for it."

The son went to the watch shop, returned, and told his father he was offered 100 bucks because it was so old.

The father then asked him to try the pawn shop next.

The son went to the pawn shop, returned, and told his father that he was offered only 20 bucks, because the watch was all scuffed up.

The father then asked him to try the museum next.

The son returned and told his father that the museum offered him a million bucks for it, because it was so rare and valuable, and they were going to display it in the rare jewelry and artifact section of the museum.

The father said, "My son, I wanted you to know that the right people in the right place will value you in the right way. Don't find yourself in the wrong place and start to doubt your value. You belong where people know your worth, because they appreciate you and know your true value."

Say goodbye to those who don't know your value, those who put you down, those who make you doubt yourself, because they'll treat you according to the value they place on you!

Once you're in a relationship that's worthy of you, you can invest in making it juicier, by focusing on intentionality.

A goddess swears by intentionality, since it's the equivalent of bringing your A game – on steroids no less – to take a relationship off the charts in hotness. She doesn't see the point otherwise.

13. Intentionality

Connecting with our lovers is all about understanding our needs, their needs, what fires relationships up, and intentionally and mindfully investing in all three.

When we plan for that first date, we put our best foot forward. We intentionally try to look our best – we may try out multiple outfits before picking one – we focus on the possibilities, and we long to connect.

Some of us wonder if there will be that first kiss at the end of the night, others do everything in their power to carry out a full on seduction, still others dream of the magic of that first "accidental" brush of skin against skin, that can take your breath away and practically give you a coregasm.

The intentionality of that early stage, known as limerence, can bring us to life in unparalleled ways, because we enjoy being turned on – in fact, we make it a priority. But somewhere along the line, we stop noticing our partner as a gift, we stop listening to them, we stop paying attention to our body's longing for them, and some even start to use sex as coinage to reward and punish – the latter is like throwing out the baby with the bath water. But all that leads to a disengagement with our own sensuality, even though we long to feel that rush of butterflies once again.

To me, it's a crime to let all that go. Remember this is the person you hoped would be drawn to you, want to date you, eventually commit to you? You anticipated each stage with bated breath. Why then did you stop the intentionality that elevated each stage to a new height, filled with planning, anticipation, excitement and gratitude?

When we're in that ethereal head space, we allow our pussy – aka the little head – to be in charge, because it simply won't allow the static in the big head to take over. So we get wet with anticipation, we have electric excitement coursing through our veins, and we focus on the delicious. In other words, we're intentionally turned on; and we can turn anyone on who intentionally crosses our path.

I know that whenever my mind is focused on ravishing and being ravished, I have pep and swagger in my walk, mischief in my eyes, and a smile that makes you wonder what I'm up to. And when people see me in that state, they smile back at me, because that's what our mirror cells are designed to do. This is why we end up smiling when we watch someone on TV smiling at us.

Our mirror cells can multiply the good, the bad, and the ugly, by reflecting back whatever they experience. It's such an exact science that the FBI uses trained professionals to access emotions in high-stakes situations, simply by allowing the mirror cells to do what they were designed to do, and then paying attention to the emotions which come up.

It's almost like reaping what you sow. If you intentionally shower your partner with attention, affection, and sensuality, they'll delight in it and want to pay you back ten-fold. But if you are disinterested, disengaged, disenchanted, they'll become disinterested, disengaged and disenchanted with you.

So rather than worrying about how the other party will see us, we can *influence* how they see us by how we see ourselves – the intoxicating thoughts in our mind, and whatever else we want them to experience with us. It's all about intentionality.

Another place where intentionality plays a big part, is in allowing us to be vulnerable. I realize that takes a lot of courage, especially if we have trust issues, but without vulnerability there is no intimacy. We have to choose it, or the choice will be made for us by default – via disengagement.

We are the creators of our own stories; our lovers are our invited guests who can partake in those stories. If we treat them right, they'll never want to leave, but we have to intentionally host an experience that's delightful for the both of us, drenched in intimacy and sensuality, that speaks to the visceral and makes us feel each other in the depths of our cores.

When our lovers enter our stories in sensual ways, they're truly vulnerable to us, exposed, in our hands, trusting us with the most intimate parts of themselves. We mustn't take that for granted. We need to cherish and celebrate every infinitesimal detail. We need to show up with the intention to connect and allow ourselves to be equally vulnerable.

Like a fight that heats up when both parties become more and more involved, passion can heat up beyond our wildest dreams, if both parties are equally engaged. It's like two mirrors facing each other, creating that mirror in mirror in mirror image effect, that multiplies everything as far as the eye can see.

But we need to intentionally *choose* to enjoy the moment, our partner, and our body's hunger, via attunement, and let mirroring take care of the rest; because that's where the connection lies. Anything short of that can become a disconnected experience – with the self and another, because mirroring is equally effective in *both* directions.

With connection comes the deep experience of being cared for, when we allow another into our core, fully and whole-heartedly.

Most men enjoy bringing a woman to the brink of pleasure, and take a great deal of pride in it. But she needs to be present, engaged, excited about every move and sensation that's geared towards her pleasure, and communicate that to him – it's a great turn on for both parties. Without that, a man can feel rejected and start to hold back, because he wants to feel like an invited guest, not an intruder.

A man cannot bring it on full-force, without knowing the impact he has on a woman. As Jada Pinkett-Smith put it:

How is a man to recognize his full self, his full power, through the eyes of an incomplete woman? ... The truth is, woman is the window to a man's heart and a man's heart is the gateway to his soul.

To connect at a mind, body, and soul level, with the self and another, we have to fully engage the mind, body and soul. And that takes intentionality!

The more you pour into a healthy partner, the more they want to give back to you. I've had hundreds of men tell me of the joy they experience in being able to give to their partner, turn her on and satisfy her, and see her happy in insurmountable ways. They're truly invested in her, but she needs to hold the space to make them feel equally wanted, desired, cherished, giving each other the permission to be sexual without judgement, so they can expand their sexual repertoire and experience new heights as a couple.

Toward that end, you can create a sexy message for your lover. Tell them exactly how you're going to ravish them and how you'd like to get ravished by them. Record it on your smart phone and listen to how you sound – the hunger should be so obvious that it turns *you* on. Do it again and again if need be, until your voice is drenched with desire, and your pussy approves.

If you don't know what you want, write an erotic story where the two of you are protagonists. It's just a fantasy so there are unlimited possibilities. Go crazy. Think about your favourite movie scenes or erotic passages – the stuff that takes your breath away – and insert yourself in the place of the hero or the heroin. Push your limits and keep embellishing until pussy responds by getting you hot and bothered.

And that's what intentionality is all about – bringing together desire and thoughtful planning. With men, it can be especially important, since sex represents different things at different times.

A man may want sex more often than a woman because it serves more needs for him – feeling wanted, validated, affirmed, emotionally intimate, soothed via touch. When those needs are met, he feels like he's in heaven. Which is why a guy can have the worst day but feel everything is copasetic in his lover's arms; whereas a woman generally needs everything to be copasetic before she wants to end up in his arms, because she's likely already connected to others in many ways before she even laid eyes on him.

In other words, the man's higher appetite isn't always just about sex; a woman needs to know that so she doesn't take away from the intimacy that he's trying to forge, by assuming he's merely objectifying or using her.

Again, it's all about intentionality, which focuses on the moment instead of getting distracted by assigning erroneous meanings, because that negative chatter can kill a wonderful opportunity.

This especially applies to different sexual interests and proclivities. Think of it like food. Some like it spicy while others enjoy subtle, some like it meaty while others vegan, some love messy sauces others crispy textures – well you get the picture. So if it's legal and consensual, there's no room for judgement, just preferences. But if someone's dealing with trauma or triggers, that has to be respected above all else.

If your lover's sexual palate feels unfamiliar, there's no harm in trying out different cuisines, starting with a little taste. If it's too spicy you can tone it down, just like adding bread when something feels too hot. But if after all that, you don't care for it, that's fine also. Point being, it's always easier for us to try on something new within reason, than to expect a partner to give up a favourite flavor. Which is not to say that you should force yourself to do something that'll trigger you, turn you off, or make you sick; it just means play within your limits and try out different things for size.

Some of the most pleasurable things I've experienced happened quite by accident, a little bit outside of my comfort zone; things that I wouldn't have ordered off the menu for myself, but reaching over to my lovers plate because something looked too delish to pass up, made me change my mind in a hurry.

What we crave gets hard-wired into us in our childhood, based on our first arousing experience, almost like imprinting. The chances of that being the same for two people are rather slim, as is the chance of two people having the same appetite.

In Annie Hall, Woody Allen and Diane Keaton play a couple that goes to see a shrink for their sexual problems. The shrink takes turns interviewing them. Woody's character is really upset that she rarely wants to have sex, just "three times a week". Diane's character reports that he wants to have sex all the time, "three times a week." It's all in our perspective – neither is right or wrong, they're just different.

A great way to find out what you like and what your partner likes is by downloading the yes-no-maybe list for sex. From mild to wild it lists all sorts of delicious stuff, with varying intensities and frequencies. You'd me amazed at what your pussy will nudge you to put on the list.

Don't be shy; this is definitely one of those times that you should be paying attention to her.

It's also a great way to make desires known without the onus being on either party, leading to awkward questions.

I hope you can get excited about opening yourself up to countless possibilities – sex should never feel dull or boring, even if your palate is vanilla.

Learn to relax your mind as soon as it starts to wander, so you can be fully engaged and present, ready to give and receive immeasurable pleasure – the kind you get through limerence when you refuse to focus on anything but the sheer good fortune of being with each other, playfully and passionately.

Putting the play back in foreplay makes it fun and adds that childlike curiosity where we can go as far as our imagination will take us. Being open to each other's desires in that manner can be beyond exciting, because we get to be whomsoever we want to be, make-believe or otherwise.

Hollywood bedrooms may be about location, location, location, with a team of experts choreographing non-replicable scenes, to capture theater of the mind. Your bedroom should be about intention, intention, intention, because that's where the sensual goddess emerges gloriously in her fullness, ready to make each experience memorable.

We'll be going over various ways to make that happen, with tips from various pleasure chests worldwide – including mine. Being the recipient of your intentionality and dedication towards making them happy, will make any lover feel like they're the luckiest person alive, because they've hit the relationship lottery jackpot!

And, they'll likely reciprocate because they'll want to keep the adventure going, which will multiply like crazy when both of you throw yourselves into that, intentionally and passionately.

14. Gender Differences

Two-thirds of our relational problems cannot be resolved, many of which tie into gender differences in one way or another, since it's like speaking two different languages. And increasing the volume doesn't help any more than speaking loudly to a foreigner does, in a language that they don't understand.

From boardrooms to bedrooms, understanding and successfully negotiating those gender differences can facilitate just about any liaison. Herewith, top ten gender differences that influence most relationships by and large – of courses there are *always* exceptions to every rule!

Top Ten Gender Differences

1.   Why We Communicate: Women believe in rapport talk, men in report talk – i.e., women talk to connect, men to convey information. I can't tell you how many couples I've seen, where she claims that he just sits there and doesn't care to talk with her, while he says, "I have nothing to say – what do you want me to say!" If he has nothing to add, he truly has nothing to say.

2.   How We Communicate: There are three primary differences.

- Women use twice as many words as men in a given day, since they like to think out loud and talk through things. Men are more direct and to the point, so they often get lost and frustrated when a woman conveys a lot of information, and can miss the point entirely.

155

- Women transmit a lot of communication between the lines; men have nothing between their lines. But since each party assumes that the opposite gender communicates exactly the way they do, women try to read between men's lines and plant stuff that isn't there; and men completely miss what's between the women's lines. Needless to say, this causes a lot of misunderstandings.

- What makes it even more challenging is, since women have a hard time asking for favours, they do so indirectly. So when a woman says, "Would you like to do such and such" what she means is "Let's do such and such". Men equate the former to someone asking their opinion and the latter to direct instruction; so they feel "no" is a legit answer when given a choice. Of course this just infuriates women since they feel dismissed by a flat out refusal to their polite request.

3. **What We Communicate About:** Being action oriented, most guys like to talk about sports, how things work, performance, ability, fixing things, etc. Being people centered, women love to talk about people, relationships, philosophy, and finding ways of being more supportive. I've had many furious women share that their partner has a bigger reaction to sporting events than sick relatives or divorcing friends, which is interpreted as him not caring. As stated before, guys will talk only when they have something to comment on in a given situation – yes, armchair coaching counts.

4. **What Drives Us:** Men are goal-oriented:, women are process oriented. A guy will not attempt anything unless he knows there's a chance of succeeding; and then, he'll try to find the fastest way to achieve his goal. A woman will not be afraid of attempting something without a specific goal, as long as it allows her to explore new possibilities and/or ensure that everyone's feeling good.

A man's goal oriented nature also extends into arguments. When a couple starts to go around in circles, the man feels there's no point, since there doesn't appear to be a clear-cut goal; and even when there is, if he doesn't get it or he doesn't have a shot at winning, he stops and goes on to do something else. It doesn't mean he doesn't care, he just doesn't see the point; but this is really hurtful to women, because they feel dismissed when they're still really upset.

5.   How We Focus: Compared to the male brain, the female brain has a lot more connections across the two hemispheres, and their neurons have a significantly farther reach. This allows women to multi-task, and men to have sharper focus on one thing at a time. It ties into the hunter-gatherer mentality, because focusing on too many things at once could distract a hunter in a way that could cost him his life in the jungle. As such, when a man has to focus on something, his brain needs to shut off to everything else. He truly can't hear when he's watching TV, reading, on his smart phone, or working on something. FYI, this extends into relaxation time as well. When men are relaxing, 70% of their brain shuts off, when women are relaxing, over 90% of their brain stays on.

6.   How We Express Love: While we all have a primary love language that we use to express love – words of affirmation, acts of service, touch, quality time, gifts – women have an easier time showing love by saying the right words, men by doing things (remember his action-oriented nature?). If you want to please your partner, the golden rule definitely doesn't apply. Best thing to do: find out their love language, and factor in the significance of communication vs action.

7.   Why We Have Sex & How It Impacts Mating: Sex is about pleasure, connection, being desired, etc. with women; for men, it fulfils those purposes in addition to tons more; which is why a guy may want sex more often than a woman, not just because of his likely higher sex drive. Among other things, it's validating, comforting, reassuring, makes him feel significant and desired, makes him feel cared for, and so on. A woman must never assume that guys are just horn-dogs, objectifying them to get off.

Since sex can mean different things to a guy, as previously mentioned, things could be going to hell in his life, but if his partner wants to have sex with him he's okay. For most women, everything else has to feel okay before they can jump into sex, which may feel like a guilty pleasure versus something that needs to be prioritized like a necessity, if they crave it. By and large, a woman generally needs to feel emotionally connected to have sex, a guy has sex to connect.

Mating with a man can be a huge investment for a woman (20+ years if she gets pregnant), but not so much for a man. So when she puts out a mating call, she can take a long time showing interest (up to 45 minutes) while she assesses his mate potential, whereas a guy can do a yes-no assessment at first site. This is why a man can often over-estimate a woman's interest in him, while a women can under-estimate his interest in her.

8.   How We Deal with Our Problems: When women have a problem, they feel better talking about it and supporting each other. Men rarely feel better talking about their problems and prefer to be left alone to find a solution to deal with a disappointment on their own; if they're at a low point, they don't want witnesses. So if he pulls away or is in a bad mood, it's his problem – she shouldn't make it hers and add to it

9.   How We Feel About Getting Help: When men are in a jam, they want to be left alone to figure things out for themselves; they'll discuss it only if they need help. When women are in a jam, they like to vent. But since a guy assumes that means she wants his help, he jumps in to tell her what to do, which frustrates the heck out her, and may even offend her deeply, because she feels that he doesn't trust her to have the skillset to take care of it on her own. This always baffles men, because they're thinking, *if she didn't want my help then why did she talk to me about it?*

10.   How We Handle Our Mistakes: When either party makes a mistake, women tend to apologize and explain themselves way too much, men hardly at all. The right balance is once for each mistake. A misunderstood female will repeat herself (following him from room to room to room, if need be) until she feels understood, whereas a guy may check out once he feels there's no point – remember his goal-oriented nature?

If there's one thing that couple work has taught me, it's that while there are many things that are unique to each couple, there are gender-related similarities in every single couple, independent of race, culture, religion, socio-economic status, education, and value systems. They're so consistent in fact that I'm now convinced that gender similarities outrank all other similarities that may seem bigger on the surface. Here's an example of how gender differences can take something innocuous and spiral it out of control:

Her: Guess what? Jimmy's cheating on Donna.

Him: Hum.

Her: You don't seem surprised. Did you already know about this?

Him: Kinda.

Her: And you didn't SAY ANYTHING?

Him: What did you want me to say?

Her: How wrong it is for one thing ... unless YOU don't think it's wrong.

Him: Does it really matter what I think? ... So, how did she find out?

Her: So that's it – all you're concerned about is her finding out? ... Would YOU tell me if YOU were cheating ... or just do your best to not get found out?

Him: But I'm NOT cheating!

Her: Hypothetically speaking.

Him: Hypothetically, it's called cheating because it's kept secret.

Her: So HYPOTHETICALLY, you could be cheating RIGHT NOW, and I wouldn't know it.

Him: But I'm NOT cheating!

Her: But if you were....

Humor aside, it's clear misunderstandings can happen due to how each gender assumes the other gender feels exactly the way they do. But most individuals fair better when they recognize those moments and look at alternative explanations.

A case in point: Anger is a secondary emotion for men, in response to feeling inadequate, guilty, impotent, or feeling bad about letting someone down, and wanting to redeem themselves in their eyes. When women realize that, the next time a man gets angry, they try to look for a less obvious reason, and experience what therapists call an "aha moment", which calms them down versus causing a major reaction.

Bottom line, knowing how gender differences work can make versus break a relationship – or at the very least, save you a lot of heartache! Speaking of genders, since the next section is geared towards male lovers, please feel free to skip it if your lover doesn't identify with that gender.

15. What Men Want

In a nutshell, to make us happy. Yes, you heard me right – to make *us* happy. In as much as I hate the cliché "happy wife, happy life" most men live by it, because they didn't get the memo on how only *we* can make ourselves happy.

But hey, if someone wants to work at my happiness, particularly by servicing the sweet spot between my legs, then bring it, since we're on the same page in that case – imagine me giving you another pussy-likes-it high-five.

That said, goal driven as their nature is, sometimes they take that job so seriously that giving us anything short of a rip-roaring orgasm is taken personally. So, many women end up faking a performance, to counter-act their performance anxiety – an absolute no-no in my books. We do enough things to make others happy, why give up the one thing that our body was especially designed for?!

So relax, let him try harder, but work with him. The whole reason that our clitoris is so mysteriously hidden is because it's a gift only for he/she who persists in pleasuring her, without pressure. Oops, there I go again, distracted by *our* needs, versus *his* wants.

In any case, having hosted a nightly, call-in show on talk radio for guys, with hundreds of interviews leading up to each topic, not to mention listening to thousands of guys share their needs/wants/wishes with me during sessions, I was amazed by how men are a lot more focused on us than we realize.

Not only do men wanna make us happy, they go to extremes to avoid making us unhappy – women have no idea how much power they have, even over powerful, successful men.

A case in point: I was invited to a celebrity party where I noticed Harvey Keitel discreetly checking me out. I walked over to say hello, because he seemed to be sitting at the bar by himself. The minute I got there, whipped as he sounded, he asked me to get away from him, because if his wife saw him talking to someone who looked as hot as me, he'd be in serious trouble. I wasn't trying to pick him up, just enjoying some star-gazing; but the way he reacted, you'd think that I was giving him a blowjob and he didn't want to get caught *in flagrante delicto*. Obviously I stepped away before giving him a panic attack, or for that matter upsetting his wife – which a goddess will never do!

Point being, time and time again I hear stories where guys go to extremes to avoid even innocent gestures, per chance they be misunderstood, and upset their partner. You think media is unjust to females? It's at least as brutal with males, giving them a bad rap, based on what *some* men do.

So, allow me to set the record straight, by sharing some top themes around what I learned.

Common Themes Regarding What Men Want

1. Men love passionate and enthusiastic women! It's pretty obvious that it makes for some pretty hot sex, but it's not just about that; they also love women who are passionate about life in general, which shows engagement.

2. Men like confident women – it's really sexy, both in and out of the bedroom. A Babe In Total Control of Herself is worth pursuing, because she moves to her own rhythm, which makes men wanna chase her all the more – it's in their hunting nature. Men hate insecure women, so do whatever it takes to get rid of those insecurities, for your own sake as well as his; he can't fix those – make that, he *won't* fix those, because he'll be too busy chasing after the confident woman. What's even more unattractive is a woman who plays the victim – so don't go there either, because in all honesty, *nobody* likes her.

3. Men love playful spontaneous women, who love to tease, play, go with the flow, and don't like to play games. They're just as comfortable with beer and wings as they are with fine dining; and they're not finicky, because they love surrendering to the moment and getting caught up in it.

4. Men love great conversationalists. They love the witty repertoire, rolling with sarcasm, not taking things too seriously, and not personalizing anything that wasn't meant that way. They also want the woman they're with to be engaged and hold her own in a conversation, versus agreeing with everything they say, or trying to one-up them. But if he expects you to not have an opinion, run!

Furthermore, men don't mind being influenced, if you have the conversation skills to negotiate. And this holds true even for most traditional men. I love the scene in the movie *My Big Fat Greek Wedding*, where Tula, the main character, tearfully complains to her mom about dad's influence over her, as the head of the household; to which the mother replies, "A man may be the head, but a woman is the neck. And the neck can turn the head any way it wants to." Point being, you have more influence than you realize, provided you play it right, despite all the BS the patriarchal society has told you.

Most men that I've worked with don't want to upset their partner, so they're generally willing to be influenced, even if they make it appear otherwise. Personally, I believe females are born with the power of persuasion. So be sure to practice that power everyday, in small doses, with different men, to gain confidence for when you really need it.

5. Men like exciting women, who love to make plans, initiate sex, and not expect them to do all the work. Even when they're not with them, they know that those women don't sit around the house moping, they're probably out there enjoying their life to the max. So they try to capture their heart before somebody else does, because such women are always surrounded by opportunities and can pick and choose what they want. If I see my girlfriends having more fun than moi, I don't struggle with FOMO, nor do I wait to be invited, I get in on the plans, because I love leading an exciting life. I'm in the process of making a second bucket list, because I've crossed off most items on my first one.

6. Men like women who take care of themselves – we're not talking high maintenance, just well-kempt. If she makes an effort, it shows that she cares about herself. This has nothing to do with how pretty, how skinny, how fashionable she is, it's about her owning her body and presenting it with pride. But remember, if you're doing that for him, you can ask him to do the same for you as well, in all fairness – think manscaping. Most women hate a man bush, particularly if he expects her to spend time down there; it's coarse, there's nothing cute about it, it's in the way, it can gag you, having pubes stuck between your teeth during sex is super-distracting, and let's face it, nobody likes ball-sweat. Pardon my ignorance, if hairy balls are indeed a bonafide fetish – I love you, accept you, and admire you.

7. Men love women who are happy, because they don't have to worry about being responsible for their happiness. Since happiness is a choice, independent of our circumstances, if we can commit to it, not only will our own demeaner change, it'll infect everyone around us as well. Warren Beaty had committed to being a perpetual bachelor, but when he met

Annette Benning, he had to marry her, because she refused to be unhappy.

8. Men love a good kisser because it signals that she'll be good in the sack – works in the other direction as well, with men who know how to kiss well. It also allows us to taste and smell each other, not to mention, swapping spit is known to share a lot of biological information which ties into compatibility. If you're wondering, but what if he's playing tonsil hockey with his tongue – show him how it's done and he'll forever be in your debt.

9. Men love women who love, respect and cherish men. It's pretty obvious when a woman doesn't like men, hard as she might try to disguise it. It's equally obvious when a woman loves men – generally because she grew up with at least one great man in her household. Those women show it through simple day to day gestures – like how they sandwich their requests between praise and gratitude, capturing the essence of love, respect, and appreciation. And what person in their right mind wouldn't want to keep that going, even if meant stepping out of their own comfort zone? Without that, every request comes across as nagging – considered to be the equivalent of slowly bludgeoning a relationship to death – obviously, nobody likes that.

10. Men love women who love themselves, because how can one love another if they don't love themselves. So know your worth, love and respect yourself, and he'll follow suit.

Are you getting the message here? Even when it's about them, it's really more about you living a fabulous life. How hard is that? All you have to do is, check in with your goddess regularly, and make sure your pussy concurs – two heads being better than one, especially when everybody's focussed on you living your best life, fully, passionately, and deliciously. Trust me, you'll both be happier for it!

Since we're now moving onto pleasuring a male partner, more or less in a straight relationship, if it doesn't apply to your lover, skip ahead. And just to be clear, these are merely tips that many women have asked me for – I get invited to speak on those more often than just about anything else – they're NOT to get you to surrender to men as their sex slaves, unless that does something for you. If anything, they're intended to help you enslave them to your Pussy Power, but only if that's something that *you'll* enjoy as well, not as a manipulative tactic!

16. Pleasuring Your Man

Over the years, I've had hundreds of couples share with me, how things started out really hot and heavy, but aren't remotely close to that any longer.

Digging deeper, I often find a common thread – most of these people treated getting married as their big goal, not a beginning. While I can understand how that might happen, after that long cycle of meeting someone, waiting for that first phone call, dating, falling in love, getting serious, etc. etc., what I have a hard time with is, viewing getting married as the big climax. If that were the case, everything else which follows would be "anti-climactic" so to speak. Being rather fond of climaxes myself, I decided to dedicate myself to helping people achieve a lifetime of blissful intimacy.

As unique as our thumbprint, as set as our personality, the triggers for desire and arousal are wired to go off in specific, individual ways. Our tastes are what they are – from favourite colours to favourite ice-cream flavours, favourite TV shows to favourite sexual preferences. Understanding and respecting our lovers' tastes and wiring is thereby critical to taking them beyond satisfaction to ecstasy, beyond their dreams and fantasies to reaching nirvana. And that's just a small part of the equation which allows us to connect in exquisite ways.

There are many erotic experiences available to us, provided we're willing to let go of our inhibitions, tune into our minds and bodies, and trust our partners enough to let them in. It will help expand our definition of sexuality to include the kind of excitement and connection that only intensify with time, as we feel safer and safer with each other.

Good sex isn't just a physical thing, it's what lovers bring out in each other. It's what happens when there's trust to share desires without recrimination, a total acceptance which encourages vulnerability and an openness to let things happen without holding back. Each experience begins with hours of teasing and an expression of cravings and intention, and ends with laying in each others arms, full of gratitude, anticipating the next encounter. Such a connection maintains that perpetual high that's similar to limerence, when we first start out; only now it energizes you like Tantra, versus depleting you like the initial chaotic urgency.

But both parties need to be present to each other, in the right head space without resentment or holding back, and attuned to their bodies' longings. Once they are free to fully let go, their hormones will pitch in to do the rest, creating an experience that's as exciting as riding a roller-coaster, from high to mellow, and everything in between.

So do whatever it takes to get *yourself* in the right head space, engage your *own* sensuality by connecting with your pussy, and *then* think about his sens-uality – aka stimulating his senses the right way, to create the most sens-ual experience for him.

Taking Care of His Senses

1.   **Smell:** Smell is the most primal instinct when it comes to sex, and it builds the strongest sense memory. Many people tend to grab scented candles to create ambiance. While I love candles and what they do for creating a magical atmosphere, scented candles are a no-no, since you want his sense memory to be attached to *your* smell, not the candles. The other reason they're a bad idea is, as they heat up, they start to feel heady

and nauseating, making 85% of men lose their erection, by activating the wrong part of the brain.

FYI, his nose isn't just good for accessing smell, it's also the way he senses your natural pheromones – known to play an important part in seduction and attraction. In scrubbing, waxing, deodorizing, we often do away with powerful signals that are programmed to attract and mesmerize, so it's important to find other ways of allowing access to those. One way that works really well is as follows: after you freshen up, think sexy thoughts, and then dab your pussy juice onto your pulse points, just like perfume. You won't need much, and you won't be able to smell it, but it works its magic on him nonetheless, without him ever realizing what hit him.

When I first heard that, me and my girlfriends decided to test out the theory. We went to one of those clubs where the same clusters of men stand in the same corners, every single weekend. As expected, they checked us out, but didn't make any moves. Following Saturday, we went back there, after dabbing on the goods, dressed identical to the previous week, right down to the shade of lipstick – this was a double-blind "scientific" experiment after all, so we couldn't have any additional variables. This time, we couldn't keep them away – they tried to overdose us with drinks, dances, and dry-humping. But don't take my word for it, try it out for yourself! Previous veterans from my classes did just that and swear that they'll never ever leave the house again, without "getting their dab on" thanks to remarkable, life-altering results.

This is also a great way to add chemistry to a sagging relationship that has lost its spark, since chemistry is about chemical reactions after all.

2.   Sound: While romantic mood music may be Hollywood's idea of a perfect seduction, it can hinder men during intercourse. Keep it soft and vocal-free, or you'll risk him "singing" along in his head – he won't be able to fight the distracting ear worm at that point, no matter how hard he tries. Furthermore, it'll activate the wrong part of the brain, making it truly challenging for him to stay hard.

Erotic words, on the other hand – picked by 97% of men as the number one aphrodisiac – engage the right part of the brain, in the right way. How else do you think a multi-billion-dollar telephone sex industry can survive, despite the free porn that's out there? Without words and sounds, the whole experience can feel like watching an amazing movie on mute.

The right words also allow us to share our fantasies, and ask for what we want, when he won't stop and ask for directions. But you have to do it the right way, using your huskiest voice – since it mimics the testosterone-rich, oxygen-deficient voice of arousal. Something like, "Ohmigosh, a little higher and you'll take me right over the edge – sure beats "a bit to the right ... darn, you almost had it", which will kill the mood by making him feel criticized. So, until a GPS is invented that says, "Move forward half an inch, now turn right" I strongly suggest that you master the craft. If you don't know where to start, begin by using food words. If you say, "Would my juicy peach ever love a juicy lick from you", he'll get the point and your peach will get licked.

With respect to sharing fantasies, erotic talk can take that to a whole new level, in a fun and harmless way. Our fantasies are what they are – we can't change them – so it's important to accept them and have fun with them. A lady I once saw was mortified by the fact that every time she made love to her husband, she thought of Denzel Washington. I reassured her that it was perfectly normal, and that it would only become an issue if she was doing Denzel, while thinking about her husband.

3. Touch: When it comes to touch, there are three key points to remember:

- With the skin being the largest sex organ, make sure you indulge it in numerous ways. Sucking, nibbling, stroking, and any other form of stimulation you can think of, causes an increase in circulation. That in turn increases sensitivity in the area, making everything feel at least twice as good.

- Touch along a curvy line is always more delicious than touch along a straight line, since nerve endings expect the pathway of a straight touch, but tingle like mad with anticipation of a curvy touch, which may or may not make it their way. And of course the increased surface area of the curvy touch is an added bonus.

- Some nerve endings are touch and pressure sensitive, others are temperature sensitive. Work both by using ice-cubes and minty things to cool down, and warm breath to heat previously cooled areas.

Caution: While minty things can do wonders for a guy, stay away from anything with menthol in it, when it comes to your pussy, because you could become severely inflamed. I found out the hard way.

One of the perks of being a sex educator is all the perky creams they give you to hand out as samples. Being the responsible teacher that I am, not to mention the horniest guinea pig on the planet, I always make sure that I test out the goods on my own pink parts first. This one time, the drug rep didn't hand me the goods until moments before I was to start facilitating a workshop. Quietly, I snuck out to the ladies room – without having a chance to check out the ingredients – applied the goo to my pussy, washed my hands, and returned to the classroom, right in time for my intro. I was anticipating my pussy to start mamboing any minute, and was rather looking forward to it. But what I hadn't realized was, the dang cream contained menthol; so just like the aphrodisiac known as the Spanish Fly, it worked by inflaming and thereby engorging the whole area, to create greater sensitivity. Trust me, no amount of pussy action is worth that!

4.   Taste: When it comes to taste, how our nether zones taste and smell often goes way beyond the cleanliness factor to, diet, degree of hydration, medication and anti-histamine use, stress, alcohol consumption, diet, and so on. If a bath doesn't do it, change the taste and smell by adding a new one. Corn syrup before going down on him, or for that matter a flavored condom, can both work wonders – the latter even contains his spunk afterwards, and is obviously critical if you're not fluid-bonded. No honey – it's too runny, so it'll end up in his butt crack, and you'll have to fish it out. No whipped cream – it dissipates too easily. Nothing oil based – it can deteriorate toys and condoms. Nothing petroleum based – it's perfect breeding ground for bacteria. No putting of anything sugary inside of you – you'll risk a yeast infection in areas where he's entirely safe.

Bottom line, it's always better to change tastes and smells, instead of avoiding certain acts. Speaking of changing tastes, if you do have the luxury of planning ahead, pineapple, strawberries and kiwi fruit make him taste better, as will avoiding garlic, onion, asparagus, artichokes and strong spices. To clarify his spunk, he can eat raw celery.

5.   Sight: Being visual creatures, men love the right visual stimuli, from how you're dressed, to how you prepare the room, to how you get his attention. That said, if you're worried about how you look naked, don't; it's a big turn-on for him. So leave the lights on, revel in your sensuality and have a great time. But if you're still thinking "no way" then throw some red scarves around all the lamps that are turned on, and you'll turn yourself on with what you see – or don't see, for that matter. Exotic dancers love to have red spotlights on them, because they create a soft focus that acts as a flaw minimizer – no bumps, no lumps, no stretchmarks. Red is also the subliminal color for arousal, hence, red light district, the scarlet letter, and red roses mark the territory. How about creating your own red-light district?

Beyond his visual nature is his equally powerful, goal-oriented nature. Combine a strip with a tease and you'll take care of both – full instruction in Appendix A. Next, you get to strip him!

Key Erogenous Zones in the Male Anatomy

1.   Lips: Guys love a good kisser – lip-o-suction is a lot more important than liposuction, as far as they're concerned. And why wouldn't it be, considering that our lips are the closest in construction to our genitals, and just as excitable! Humans were programmed to kiss, since kisses convey a lot of information – physical and emotional – small wonder we're the only species with our lips on the outside of our mouths. Furthermore, studies show that couples who take just 10 seconds to kiss before they part ways in the morning and another 10 seconds when the come together at the end of the day, are infinitely more connected, as reflected in their extremely lower divorce rate, all other things being equal.

2.   Nipples: Most men love to have their nipples sucked, squeezed and played with. But start gentle and increase intensity and pressure only if he's digging it and he can take it. And if he really likes it, make sure you give him proper lip service. Most men have one nipple that's more excitable – it's the one that gets erect first – especially pay attention to that one if your other hand is busy elsewhere. But just like women, not all men will get excited by nipple play; so if it isn't his thing, there are a lot of other areas that you can concentrate on.

3.   Penis: A penis is extremely sensitive – both physically as well as emotionally. Physically, even though the entire thing feels wonderful, most men say that the higher up you go, the more sensitive it feels.

Within the penis itself, there are many additional parts to it. There's the shaft, which leads to the highly excitable head – the glans. Within the head, the meatus (opening at the top), the fraenulum (peak like junction), and the corona (the ridge at the bottom of the head that makes it look like a helmet) are the most sensitive parts on the penis.

FYI, a circumcised penis is more delicate than an un-circumcised one, with respect to how much rough play it can handle.

At a psychological level, for men, the size and appearance of their genitals is generally their most significant physical concern; for women, the size and appearance of everything else. We need never say, "Look, Becky, it's a whole inch ... and isn't it pretty?" His six inches on the other hand, never resemble a sex inch vibrator.

With that in mind, no cutesy names or penis jokes. Besides, dick jokes are never as funny as pussy jokes anyways; think Justin Timberlake's Dick in a Box vs Wanda Sykes' detachable pussy – both are pretty funny, but Wanda definitely takes the cake. Furthermore, dick jokes are like racial jokes – you can make fun of your own, but everyone else is off limits and highly inappropriate, no matter how harmless it may appear. Trust me, "some of my best friends are dicks" won't get you off the hook! Sorry, I digress, but I wanted to make the point of how sensitive guys can be, about their genitals.

Beyond the vanity is the penis's functionality; the drink and drive ban also applies to drinking and driving each other wild – one to two drinks tops, within two hours prior to sex, is all that a man can handle, if he is to get it up and keep it up.

4.   Balls: Balls love to be licked and sucked gently, but never being pulled apart or crushed together – hence the sack is referred to as a single unit. If he's too hairy, suggest he go sans, not just because of my previous hairy ball comments, but also because it'll make it all the more pleasurable for him, make his mini me look an inch longer, and make your job infinitely easier, which is why most men nowadays believe in manscaping. My single friends say that they're shocked when one doesn't. But if he's not game for that, run your fingers through the hair to dislodge the loose ones, and then lick his balls in the direction of the hair growth to settle down his crotch 'fro. FYI, it's perfectly okay to say that there will be a lot more licking without the hair than to settle down the hair, bushy ball fetish notwithstanding.

5.   Perineum: Behind his balls is his perineum – smooth, hairless area between the balls and the anus – known to be one of the most sensitive external parts on a man's body. If you stimulate it just so, you'll transport him into ecstasy. A knuckle massage, nail strumming, vibrator action, can all work.

6.   Prostate aka The Male G-Spot: Often unrecognized yet extremely sensitive spot on a man's body (most sensitive to be exact) is his prostate, often referred to as the male G-spot, located 2-3 inches inside the anus, on the tummy side. Being a highly sensitive zone (with numerous nerve endings) and being stimulated by the stronger pudendal nerve, ignoring it would be like ignoring your clitoris and G-spot (also stimulated by the pudendal nerve). His penis is only accessible to the weaker pelvic nerve – the same nerve which takes care of your vagina (hence 70% of women can't come from vaginal stimulation alone). But the sensation from having his prostate stimulated is so exquisite that once a guy tries it, chances are that he'll want more; but he's gotta try it out first. And if he's really digging it, don't read anything into it – it's just a delectable sensation, which has nothing to do with orientation. So ditch your worries and learn how to give him a proper prostate massage; you'll

175

own his body forever! If you're too squeamish, buy a butt plug and let it do the trick for you, without making either one of you uncomfortable. But whatever you do, be sure to prepare his anus properly, first – instructions to follow.

Now onto arousing those wonderful parts!

10 Commandments for Male Arousal

Arousal is what connects desire to pleasure to orgasm – one of the most gender-specific parts of sexuality. For example, since the male brain is programmed to focus on one task at a time, in a goal-oriented way, when he's into sex, he's really into sex and not thinking about much else. On the other hand, the female brain is designed for multi-tasking, so she can bring many things into the sack with her, even when she's super excited about sex.

If you wanna arouse him just so, be sure to follow his biology, not yours. Herewith, some additional tips to help you get *both* his heads to cooperate, so you can take his arousal off the charts.

1.   Stroke his ego before you stroke his libido. Praise his positive qualities just as you like yours praised. Make him feel good about who he is. Appreciate him often, and appreciate him like you would nobody else. When men stray, most often it's because someone made them feel special, when they'd stopped feeling that way at home.

2.   Just as you wouldn't want him to only stroke your favorite part, pay attention to all of his body parts, not just his penis. Play with all the parts that we discussed, along with his back, his glutes, the area on his neck where his beard ends, and everything else that has him moaning. But you have to explore to find out what he likes, and how he likes it – ask him to show

you, experiment with different sensations, temperatures, and textures, use your sensual expertise from part A, and so on.

3.   Although male skin is thicker than female skin and thereby requires greater pressure for stimulation, do not be too rough with his penis. Men appreciate as much pressure as a good handshake – not too strong, not too limp.

4.   Men like a quick rush into arousal, but when you're actually in the throes of the act, break the fast and furious myth. The longer you prolong it, bringing him to the edge but not quite letting him spill over, the stronger his orgasm will be. In other words, the longer the action, the stronger the reaction. (Hint: The rise of his testicles should tell you when he's getting close.)

5.   Encourage erotic communication. If he asks you to try something out, feel good about the fact that he's asking you; do not show disgust or disapproval, since you'll put a kybosh on future erotic communication. And just because he might stop talking about it doesn't mean he'll stop craving it, because it's hard-wired like a favourite flavour. If you're not game for an idea, make it clear that it's the idea that you're uncomfortable with, not him.

6.   Mix it up; variety is the spice of life. Since the brain has a tendency to habituate, what felt good once may not feel that way in the future, particularly for men. So add variety, to keep it fresh. Have the courage to explore new things – role play, experiment with toys, games, sensual movies, and talking dirty – because good sex happens 90% in the brain and only 10% in the bod.

7.   Respect his penis. Since the size and the appearance of their genitals are a big concern for many men, let him know how beautiful/big/hard his penis is; but be authentic and don't make stuff up. You'd be amazed at what the confidence will do for him. They say women have penis envy, but the way guys

are obsessed with their penises, I always say, "Show me a guy in a locker room and I'll show you penis envy."

8.   Be sensitive to his erectile challenges. Anything from stress/anxiety, to fatigue, to alcohol, to resentment can make it very challenging for a guy to get it up and/or keep it up. But if it's an ongoing issue, it may be due to erectile dysfunction, which can often signal other medical issues – gently suggest a doctor's visit in that case. FYI, if it's a psychological issue, he'll still be able to get some nighttime and morning woods; but if that isn't happening, then it's likely a physiological problem.

9.   Respect his libido/desire issues. Men can have low desire, just like women, due to any number of reasons – resentment, medical problems, andropause, or simply a low baseline – except it's a lot harder for them to handle, since they're expected to be perpetually horny. In reality, 12% of guys can take it or leave it, and 7% would rather leave it. So if any of this sounds like your guy, don't assume it's about you, and try to discuss it in a sensitive, caring manner. FYI, stress can lead to high levels of the stress hormone cortisol and low levels of testosterone – the former can cause erectile issues, the latter can impact the libido.

10.   Take responsibility for initiating sex at least some of the time. Men need us to do that, so they can feel desirable. This is especially important if you have a lower drive than him – meet him half-way in that case, by getting things started when you feel you can get into it, focusing on how you'd *like* to feel versus how you *are* feeling.

Whatever you do, make it special and know that what you do for each other (both in and out of bed) is at least as important as who you are.

Next, I'd like to offer some suggestions to get the most bang for your buck.

7 Tips for the Action Between Your Hips

1.   The person on top gets to control the rhythm, depth of penetration, and thrusting. Female dominant positions therefore make it easier for you to come, and decrease intensity just enough to slow him down – a win-win situation. This also holds true for oral sex – particularly when it's being performed on you.

My favourite suggestion for you: have him lie comfortably on his back, pillows supporting his neck. Then straddle his face, knees on either side of his head, your body leaning into the wall or headboard just behind. This way, you can push down if you need more intensity, lift up if you need less; and you can move your hips in the direction of your choosing, while he gets to indulge you from a great vantage point, without straining his neck, and without needing to pull a tough balancing act. If his tongue is extra-skilled, have him lick the underside of your clitoral hood, while his hands reach up to your breasts if you like breast play. I know this one is for you, but most guys get quite charged up from indulging a woman in this way – so take the responsibility and do it "for him".

2.   Play with specific positions to obtain enhancement. To make yourself feel tight and his girth feel huge, choose positions where your legs are straight up in the air, since such positions will narrow out your vaginal canal. To make him feel long, choose positions where you draw back your knees toward your shoulders, while laying on your back, thereby shortening out your vaginal canal. Alternately, if flexibility is a problem, you may use a pillow below the hips of the person on the bottom – it will push him in really deep, particularly when you're on top.

3.   Tightening up the PC muscle in both men and women allows for greater sensations and better orgasmic control. This is the same muscle you squeeze when you try to keep yourself from going to the bathroom. Practice the squeeze release technique as often as you can, for as many reps as you can – remember grip-tease from part A? Once you get the hang of it, try to pull tighter and higher. This is where the elevator exercise comes from. Ladies, learn to take that elevator up three floors – tighter and higher each time – as per the instructions in part A. You'll drive each other crazy, not to mention be able to reach multiple orgasms. And the best part: you can do this exercise anywhere, anytime – while heading up a board meeting, clicking with the turn signal in your car, during an argument ....

4.   Both men and women require a steady rhythm and increased intensity to reach an orgasm. Don't go changing, trying to please each other, at that magical moment – it never works!

5.   If penetration hurts you earlier on, spend more time getting ready. The cervix flips out of the way with stimulation, the inner two-thirds of the vagina balloons, and the extra lubrication never hurt anybody.

6.   As mentioned earlier, sucking, nibbling, stroking, and any other form of stimulation that you can think of, causes an increase in circulation, which increases sensitivity. So take your time indulging his largest erogenous zone – his skin.

7. Observe the following rules for any form of anal penetration.

- Lubricate using a thicker anal lube, since it's a non-lubricating zone.

- Practice safe sex, because being a thin-walled area, it's prone to tearing and infecting easily. We're not talking STIs, we're talking about the bacteria that are indigenous to the anus but can wreak havoc elsewhere. So it's important to use a condom on anything that gets inserted in there, which should be changed before inserting it elsewhere.

- Make sure that anything that goes in either has a flange or a body attached to it – being an open-ended cavity, it will get sucked up otherwise, necessitating a trip to the emergency room.

- Relax both sphincters. The outer sphincter, being under voluntary control, can be willed into relaxation. The inner sphincter, being involuntary, needs to be relaxed manually. This is easily done by physically "training" the muscle with progressive penetration. Rule of thumb: depending upon the girth you're preparing for, insert one finger for one minute, followed by two fingers for two minutes, followed by three fingers, and so on, until you reach the girth which needs to be accommodated (all the while observing the above lubing and cleanliness rules).

Beyond all that, it's really important to take at least as much responsibility for your own orgasm as your partner's.

Far too many women only concentrate on their partner and then resent being dissatisfied themselves. Think about it, who better to make sure that your body moves in the same direction as your hope – the definition of good sex, according to sexual philosopher, Sally Tisdale.

There's no such thing as "my partner doesn't get me off" in my books; you have to show them how, because orgasms are taken not given.

Next, we're going to get into the nitty-gritties of touching him just so.

Manual Labour

To grasp his penis, use your palm and fingers (closed together) to create a comfortable grip, which will allow for a steady, up and down rhythm, like a massage. Break the fast and furious myth and stroke it slowly, gently, seductively. Use lube to slide and glide for max pleasure – unless of course you plan to go oral next, because most lubes don't taste terribly good, but Astroglide is okay.

Next, build a nice stroke-twist, stroke-twist rhythm in an up-down, up-down fashion. Basically, you stroke up the shaft, twist over the head – like opening up a jar cap a quarter turn (don't have to go too hard, he's already loosened it many times) – slide back down to the base, twist there, and start your journey back up again. With your free hand, hold onto the top of his scrotal sack, without messing with his balls, and lightly tug. It's almost as if you're milking him. (Hint: Squeezing here also helps him get hard quicker and last longer, much like wearing a cock-ring.) You can also use silk panties or a cuddly glove to polish his balls, or a finger vibe to make them quiver with pleasure.

Next, I'd like to get into some variations – my friends and I playfully refer to them as "ten tips to play with dicks".

1.   The Ring Exercise: A great way to increase the circulation in a penis that has erectile challenges is by doing the ring exercise. Form a ring around the base of his penis with your thumb and index finger. Tighten and release the ring for one second at a time, with greatest pressure on the sides, versus front and back. Keep moving the ring up, half an inch at a time, until you get to the head.

2.   Rock & Roll & Shimmy: Another way to "warm him up" is by holding the head of the penis straight out with one hand, so it's at a 90-degree angle to his body. Then move the penis in small circles, like a joystick of a video game (easiest when he isn't rock hard). Follow five slow circles, with five fast ones, and then give his penis a little shake, like you'll playing the maracas.

3.   The Juicer: Hold the base of the shaft with one hand and pull down, so the head gets taut and the sensitivity increases. Lubricate your other hand and loosely encase the head of the penis so your fingers form a claw around it and your fingertips encircle the corona. Twist your wrist in half circles, like you're using a juicer.

4.   Penetration Fascination: Hold the base of his erect penis and pull down so the skin is taut. With the other hand – lubed – make a tight fist with a small opening, then slowly push the head through, while squeezing tightly. Just remember, the tighter your grip, the slower you should go. This mimics that exciting feeling when he first enters you.

5.   Plucking The Mushroom: Have him lie on his back, with his penis resting on his belly. Using your thumb and forefinger, gently squeeze the tissue at the base of the shaft, closest to his belly and push down slightly. This should make the shaft rise a bit from its position and point toward the ceiling. Then, while keeping your hold, knead the base of the penis in tiny circles, to stimulate greater blood flow, while the thumb and forefinger of your other hand form a ring, wrapped around the corona, lightly stroking up and down over it, giving it a little massage.

6.   The Palm Sisters: Place your generously lubed palms on either side of the shaft and start moving them in opposite directions, like you're rolling play dough. Once you get the rhythm going, have one hand moving up, the other moving down, and then switch in the other direction, so you maintain the up and down movement.

7.   Patty Cake: Flatten your hands, take the penis between them, then start slapping it back and forth, from palm to palm, as gently as possible. Once it gets rock hard, you can get a bit rougher with it – some guys like you to strum it with your nails, or drive it crazy with a finger vibe.

8.   Windshield Wiper: With him laying down, facing up, drip some warm lube below his belly button and rest his penis on it. Then place the heel of your hand firmly against the shaft, and start moving it back and forth like a windshield wiper.

9.   Victory Ride: Using your index and middle fingers, form two Vs with your two lubed hands and put them on either side of the penis. Start moving them up and down in a semi-circular motion, gently tightening your grip. If your mouth can grip the glans, all the better!

10.   Kneading: Make a fist with one hand. Without bending your wrist, place your fist up against his perineum. Begin vibrating your fist back and forth against the perineum, while your other hand slides and glides over his shaft and head.

Oral Play – 10 Tips for Creating Magic Between Your Lips

Oral sex is one of the most pleasurable sensations for a man, as it is for a woman. It's about total acceptance and extra sensations unlike much else. There is no other single act which will drive him insane, if done right – hence it leaves the most memorable impression.

If you feel weird about it, look at all the mammals out there – they wouldn't dream of getting into it without licking and sniffing the genitals first, because it creates arousal and attunement. With that mindset, let it go, let it free your body and move your soul – and his – as you try out the following oral skills.

1. To start, make sure your teeth are covered, and your suction is tight enough to dent your cheeks, similar to when you suck on a straw to access a thick milkshake. Begin by taking his entire penis into your mouth and developing an up-down rhythm, sucking with even pressure, except for when you get to the ridge just below the head – give it extra suction here, as you pull up each time.

2.   Next, vary the up and down movement by adding twists, side to side head motion, and rotating the mouth up and down like a cork screw, all the while taking it in as deep as you can. Apart from being sensations which the vagina can't provide, these moves indulge curvy moves and offer greater variety, which leads to greater excitement. And it's nice to keep the body guessing, which keeps it fully engaged.

3.   Now throw in some tongue ticklers and you'll send him through the roof. You can lick and flick the corona – the ridge beneath the head of the penis – run your tongue up and down his shaft, rhythmically flick your tongue along the length of his shaft like a finger playing the flute, and so on. Think it can't get any better? Think again.

4.   What can make these sensations even more mind-blowing is, you moving your head in one direction and your tongue in the other, exquisitely confusing and teasing his nerves even more so. It's all about licking, sucking, flicking, kissing, with all manner of variations, maintaining constant contact and rhythm, gaining speed as you go along. And your hands must always work in conjunction with your mouth, indulging other parts. In general, pay attention to what makes him moan the most and indulge him with it. This means looking at him – guys say that when a woman looks them straight in the eyes, while pleasuring them orally, it gives them an incredible rush.

5.   Another area you need to pay attention to is his balls – just before he comes, his balls will draw up pretty high. You

want to go fast and furious at that point, to intensify his release, and then ease up just as he pops his cork.

6.   Whatever you do, really get into it to make it an intense experience. If your mouth tends to get tired, switch over to your hands – go for a little palm sisters action – and then return to your mouth whenever you can. Eventually, you won't even need to switch, because practice will make it perfect. But if he wants a threesome and you don't, tell him there's always room for palm sisters. When my husband asked me if I'd ever consider a threesome, I told him, "Of course, as long as one person is doing all the housework and the other's massaging my feet!" Since then, he's constantly pleasured me by doing both.

7.   Another way to achieve intensity is, if he wants you to deep throat him, put a pinch of salt on the far back of your tongue and reverse your breathing – in through the mouth and out through the nose – you'd be amazed at how much deeper you'll be able to take him in, once you relax your throat in this way.

8.   To make it a hot and cold blowjob, slip a Listerine slip into your mouth to cool it down, while your warm breath can heat it up, to provide temperature changes. Another enhancer which makes for an even more exquisite feeling is, adding an ice-cube – best ones are custom made with sparkling water or club soda, since they'll add a tingle as well. But the very best is, remembering to pay attention to more than the penis – balls, perineum, and anus – all the while making as much eye contact as possible.

9.   The best way to be able to manoeuvre through these moves is, by having him stand in front of you, while you sit comfortably in a chair. Or you could literally eat him out by having him sit on a dining table while you sit in a dining chair in front of him and do your magic. Both of those positions will

also allow you to cater to one of the most important parts of a good blow-job – eye contact.

10.   Most men say that eye contact can make or break the experience – it's the difference between connecting with him versus chowing down on it as a duty.

I was once the resident sexpert in a reality TV series. One episode, the girls wanted to master the art of giving head. The guys in the group had created what they called an erectometer – a cardboard meter where the needle looked like a penis and the ratings ranged anywhere from soft to rocket-hard, with various gradations in between. As the girls cooed, tried to talk dirty, and showed off their techniques on dongs, the best they could rate was a chubby. Then came sexpert advice from yours truly and took it to rock hard; that is until I threw in the porn star stares – then, the erectometer started to vibrate while maintaining rocket-hard and sounded off a fire alarm. If you don't believe me, try it out for yourself; I'd be willing to bet that you'll trigger a five-alarm siren in your bedroom.

For step-by-step instruction on ten types of blowjobs, see Appendix B.

Top Ten Positions & Techniques

As sex comes out of the closet, we have access to more and more books and articles on more and more positions, that can make anyone feel a little bit overwhelmed. Women will tell me that they can only manoeuvre through ten of the positions from a top hundred list they just read; I tell them that that's eight more than I can do. Point being, there's nothing wrong with having a few favourites, depending upon what you like and what your body can manage. After all, most sexual positions are variations of the following ten themes. So pick what rocks your boat and is still doable, and play with it, adding variety by changing speed, location, and possibly adding extras, like toys and role plays.

CAT: While the traditional missionary remains a favorite with most couples, thanks to max eye contact, intimacy, and the possibility of kissing; since the woman wraps her legs around the man, it makes it less than snug, not to mention, the friction from thrusting doesn't get anywhere near her clit.

On the other hand, Coital Alignment Technique – aka the CAT position – allows a woman to squeeze her legs together, once the guy enters her, forcing his legs on the outside, to create a snugger fit. The guy then hooks his feet under hers, or pushes off a footboard if he's too tall, allowing him a chance to ride higher than usual, creating max friction against her clit, thereby increasing her chance of having a clitoral orgasm, which can be further magnified, by him rotating his hips in a screwing motion – I guess they call it screwing for good reason.

Cowgirl: As the man lays comfortably on his back, the woman can straddle him, with the bulk of her weight on her knees, either facing him or facing away from him. This position allows him to get in nice and deep, while she gets to control the rhythm, thereby her orgasm, which can be intensified if he adds in some manual stimulation, or a vibrator against her easily accessible clitoris.

But if his penis is too small, he can raise his knees and allow her a chance to slide down on his thighs and lock onto his penis – a much better angle to get him deeper inside her. To make it tighter still, he can throw a pillow or two beneath his lower back. This one's called the **slide-lock**!

Counter Solution: When penile length is an issue, any position where a woman pulls her knees and thighs back toward her chest to shorten her vaginal canal, makes him feel extra long; but if you don't give the vagina a chance to warm up first, it can hurt. This position is easily managed if you lay on a counter and he stands in front of you; but be sure to lay on something comfortable, because the counter can feel uncomfortable otherwise.

189

Spooning Dogs: The man spoons up into the woman from behind, while she pulls up her knees just enough to allow his penis good vaginal access. This position allows ample opportunity for him to stimulate her clitoris manually or play with her breasts if she likes. It's the ultimate in comfort, for both pregnant and plus size women.

Grinding Mill: We all know what the doggie looks like, but for those who love it but can't manage it, due to a significant height difference, or because her back or either of their knees can't take it, the grinding mill allows a more comfortable option.

Basically, the woman kneels into a heavy chair or sofa, leaning forward, supporting herself against the backrest, while the man stands behind her and enters her, allowing them greater flexibility to accommodate height differences, while being easy on her back and both sets of knees.

Furthermore, it allows him to spoon up into her, and kiss the erogenous zones on the back and sides of her neck, making it all the more intimate. This position is also ideal for a woman who finds the doggie to be a bit painful, since she gets to control how far back she pushes her butt, thereby the depth of penetration.

Twisted T: A great position to tighten up the fit, if she gets too wet for friction, or he's too small for a snug fit. Basically, the woman lays on her side, with her knees quite bent and upper leg slightly raised, while the guy kneels behind her butt, straddles her lower leg, and enters her vagina from beneath.

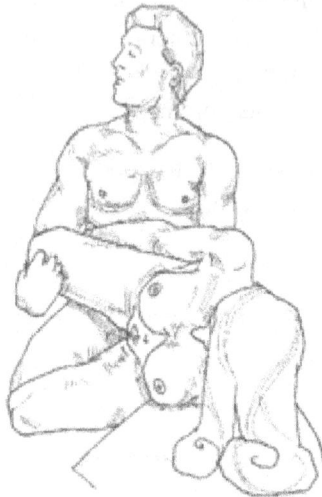

For plus size couples, **the pretzel dip** is a slightly better option, since he gets to pull apart her legs, and get a deeper thrusting angle.

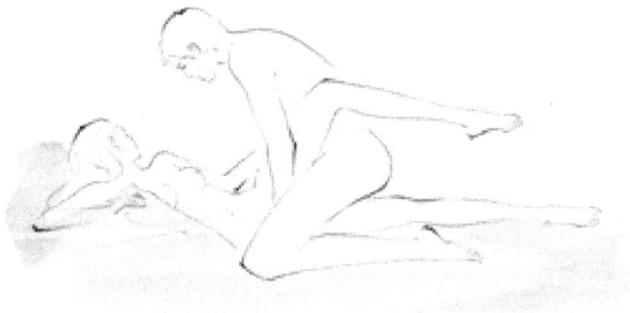

Mirror L: Any position where a woman's legs are straight up in the air, narrows her vaginal canal, making his girth feel huge and her pussy feel really tight.

Thus, mirror L is the ideal position for addressing both those issues.

The woman lays on her back and raises her legs, while he kneels close to her butt and enters her vaginally. She can then rest her legs on his shoulders, or the headboard just behind him, or put her feet against his chest.

This can be helpful if the length is an issue, as bent knees will also shorten the vaginal canal. She can increase her grip on his penis, making for an experience beyond imagine.

Lap Dance: For deep penetration, intimacy, and comfort, a man may sit on an armless chair, and the woman can straddle his lap and mount his erection. If she faces him, they can kiss, hug, and stroke each other; if she faces away, they can be seated in front of a mirror and watch themselves, while he has easier access to stimulate her breasts and clitoris.

Spooning Twiddle – a great position for the female to get all her sweet spots stimulated, since it's hands-free for both parties.

The Swing: The man sits on a bed with his legs crossed in front of him, while the woman mounts him face to face, with her legs coming together behind his back, their arms wrapped around each other. This position offers a great deal of intimacy, since you need to hold onto each other tightly for balance, support, and to get a rhythm going – via a beautiful rocking motion. The *Kama Sutra* refers to this as the lotus position.

Final word on intercourse – take your time, change the tempo, intensity or location, and don't be afraid to include some toys, to keep the play in foreplay and the life in your sex-life.

Congratulations on learning how to seduce him exquisitely, tease deliciously, connect emotionally, communicate erotically, and indulge sexually, in the most profound ways, making you the very best lover ever. All you have to do now is, give and receive pleasure without bounds or limits. And make sure he does for you at least as much as you've done for him. This is just to give you some sexy hints to enslave him, not to become his slave.

Conclusion

We've talked about discovering what fires you up and what takes away from you living the life you want.

We've also discussed how to connect with your inner goddess to get rid of whatever gets in the way, so you can live life on your own terms, unapologetically.

As well, we've talked about Pussy Power and why it's so important.

And, we've discussed how to support each other without tearing each other down.

We've talked about how to feel good about yourself – mind, body, and soul.

All this is to say, I hope by now you've awakened your inner goddess, manifested your true self, and you're ready to intentionally connect with your sensuality/sexuality, for your own sake as well as the sake of your lover(s), if you should so choose.

What I wanna add to that is, don't sweat the small stuff, just live in the moment, enjoy life to the max, and *then* you can get sweaty for all the right reasons, if you should so choose.

It's all about choices – you choose to be happy, you choose to fly solo or with a chosen lover, you choose how you want to express your sexuality, and so on.

I for one like to think of myself as 'try'-sexual – I choose to try out any and everything that appeals to me at least once, as long as it's legal and consensual.

Ultimately, I respect others, as I like to be respected myself. None of this is about me-me-me, or for that matter manipulation. It's about giving each other the permission to live and let live.

Let no one take your power away. You can willingly give it to a partner if you're dabbling in kink, but that's about power-with versus power-over, because the person handing over the power is still in charge.

Pussy Power is yours to enjoy. If you've become the woman that I hope you've become, you'll have men chasing after you in droves – think, an egg being chased after by millions of sperm, just dying to penetrate it!

Once you choose who you wanna invite into your playful, joyful, sensual inner sanctum, make sure they still respect you and your power. If they do, intentionally surrender to the delightful orgasmic stratosphere that'll take you out of orbit. If they don't, don't lose sleep over such a person; and definitely don't let them take your power away, particularly on their way out.

Ditch the analysis paralysis and sappy heart-break music, throw on some dance music, put on your dancing shoes and killer dress, and go out for a girls' night, to see that you still got it. Hunt and get chased, because they're flipsides of the same coin. It's all in your delivery.

It makes me think of the story of the sun and the wind:

On a still day, the sun and the wind were bored, so the wind said to the sun, "Let's play a game. ... You see that man in a jacket walking on the winding road below us? Whichever one of us can get his jacket off the fastest wins."

The sun smiled a knowing smile and said, "You go first, since it's your idea."

Proudly, the wind started to huff and puff, because she felt she had the power to rip the jacket off the man's shoulders, whereas the sun didn't have any such force.

But the harder the wind tried, the tighter the man fastened his buttons. The final time she huffed was at the sun, as she frowned and said, "Let's see you try!"

The sun just smiled and shone brightly, warming up the man; who then took off his jacket off his own free will.

And that's the key to making things happen – or for that matter, peeling clothes off – no force required, because people will want to surrender to your will, and see the merit in their decision.

Pussy power is just like that, *and* she can get you hot and sweaty just like the sun!

I hope I've got your juices going to listen to your pussy and expand your sexual repertoire.

If you need a little help to get your imagination going, be sure to check out the Appendix C for hot erotica penned by yours truly.

At the end of the day, I want you to treat your lovers well, and yourself at least as well – everybody wins.

Bon Voyage!

For more information, on workshops and seminars, check out: www.TalkWithRebecca.com

APPENDIX A – STRIPPING FOR A LOVER

Getting Ready for the Strip Down:

Start off by picking the music that'll provide the right pace and mood for you to move to.

Next, pick an outfit to match the music – soft and sensual for softer sounds, leather or PVC for harder sounds. Corsets need to be four inches less than your natural waist – anything more will shift things around elsewhere – and lingerie needs to be a size larger, for easy removal. And since the outfit for your night in is more important than the outfit for your night out, go crazy. Plan for lots of layers, so you can prolong the peeling.

To match the perfect outfit, you need the perfect shoes – every girl knows that. In this case, that means the highest heels you can manage, since they'll make your legs appear longer, push your butt and breasts out in the "presenting position", and make your moves more graceful and accentuated. But they need to be sized properly. Measure between the tip of your big toe and the edge of your heel; divide by two to find the best heel height you can manage, with the longest sole possible, for stability.

Once you have the perfect pair of shoes, learn to walk in them – leading from the hips, criss-crossing one foot in front of the other, as if you're being pulled by a leash that's attached to your belly button. Next, you can add accessories, to make your outfit feel like a costume, so you can slip into a new persona, one that allows you to feel uninhibited. A feather boa is a great prop and wigs and gloves a fun way to open up your repertoire.

Fun Steps to Get you Started:

1.   To begin, have two chairs facing each other, with your lover seated in one and you in the other, your legs crossed properly at the knees, in a lady-like fashion.

2.   Once the music starts, sensually slide your upper leg down the lower leg, then pry open both legs with your hands, as soon as both feet hit the ground.

3.   Thrust out your breasts twice.

4.   Move your head down to your right knee; then glide it to your left knee in a half moon, and flip your hair up as your head comes back up.

5.   Next, shoot your arms straight up in the air, one at a time, closing the corresponding legs with them.

6.   Run your hands down your body to grab the chair on either side of your butt, so you can slide down into a "*Flashdance*" position and touch yourself.

7.   Slide back up, pry open your right thigh by ninety degrees, twice, and then push off the chair into a standing position, like you're being pulled up by a leash that's attached to your heart, with your head dangling as far back as possible.

8.   Once you're standing, shake your hips from side to side, in a 2 right, 2 left, 1 right, 1 left sequence, and end with two wide booty swirls, from right to left.

9.   Walk around the chair to the back (to the count of four), with loads of attitude.

10.   Grab a hold of the back of the chair to support yourself, and swivel down in a zig zag motion to the count of four, until you're on your haunches – flash your crotch twice, by opening up your knees, and then get back up the way you came down.

11.   Go around the chair on the right side and put your right leg onto it's side, left foot planted firmly on the ground.

12.   Stroke your butt in a circular fashion with your right hand, then slap it twice, and bring down your right leg.

13.   Now push aside the chair with loads of attitude and walk up to him, criss-crossing one foot in front of the other.

14.   Stand in front of him and look at him hungrily, while you use your hands to trace your body in the shape of an hourglass; then continue moving your hands down your thighs, as you push them apart, right down to your ankles, and come back up to grab your crotch.

15.   Turn your butt towards him, do a booty shake and give him a great rear view. FYI, booty shakes are controlled at the waist, not the booty itself; and you can accentuate those by moving your feet up and down to the beat of the music, while shaking your butt as fast as you can.

You are now ready to strip, so herewith, some generic "rules".

The Art of the Striptease

1.   You can start off by pulling your lapels together and squishing your breasts. After enough boobie play, you can slide it off slowly and then discard it with an attitude. FYI, all items need to be discarded that way.

2.   Get closer to him, play with yourself, tease him, slap your ass, and do whatever else has him anticipating your next move with bated breath. You'll wanna concentrate on his favourite body parts.

3.   Constantly move, even when peeling your clothes off, ever so slowly, alternating between the top and the bottom layers. Go a-g-o-n-i-z-i-n-g-l-y s-l-o-w – just because your bra straps are off doesn't mean you'll empty your cups just yet. Once the erotic tension reaches its pinnacle, you can amp up the ante.

4.   Get really close to him, straddle his lap, put your arms around his neck (to steady yourself), and give him a lap dance.

5.   When he can't take it any longer, take his hand and slide it along the inside of your thigh – the broken rule will make the other hand reach for the second thigh. If so, gently slap that hand, move away, stop the show, point a disapproving finger at him, and then come back, after asserting your control.

6.   Pretend you're a long spoon and stir the pot – right arm straight up, left foot moving full circle around right foot, which will be your pivot point, booty sticking out sensually.

7.   As his breathing quickens, slide your hands down to his thighs (to support yourself) and push off into a standing position.

8.   Continue doing whatever makes you feel sexy – alternating between giving him some and holding back.

9.   As you get close to the end, walk away three steps – again, one foot in front of the other – stop, come back around toward him in the same way, or do a cat crawl on the floor towards him (if you're flexible enough, and if there's something on the floor to protect your knees).

10.   Finish by standing in front of him, licking your lips, and giving him a hungry come hither move, which invites him to follow you wherever you wanna take him.

It's all about teasing, until the eventual prize becomes more valuable than ever.

FYI, to ensure that he's mesmerized and hypnotized, keep him engaged at all times, by ensuring that the movement never stops, and eye contact is maintained hungrily at all times, even when you have your back to him.

APPENDIX B – TEN TYPES OF BLOW-JOBS

1.   **Cock-Screw:** Twist your mouth around his cock as you go up and down the shaft.

2.   **Popping the Cock:** As your suck up the shaft, you want to grab a hold of the head of the penis between your lips and pop it.

3.   **Tongue War:** If you take it out of your mouth, have a tongue war with the head – like the kiddy thumb wars you used to have – right against his fraenulum.

4.   **Postage Stamp:** Rub the fraenulum against the flat of your tongue.

5.   **Hummer:** Vibrate your lips (like kids do when they make a boat sound) as you grip the corona with your lips.

6.   **Dolphin:** Take his cock and bob it up and down in your mouth, like a dolphin bobbing in and out of water.

7.   **Flicking the Meat:** Grab a hold of his corona between your lips and then flick your tongue from side to side, across the tip – if you happen to dip into the meatus, all the better!

8.   **Licking Ice Cream:** Lick his cock like you would an ice cream cone, and then make the same motion with the back of your tongue as you would when you swallow something.

9.   **Playing the Flute:** Dart and flick your tongue up and down the shaft, like you're playing the flute.

10.   **The Symphony:** As you might've guessed it, it's about doing more than one thing at once – involve your hands, boobs and hair if you can, and giving him a treat of a lifetime!

The best way to be able to switch back and forth between these positions is if you sit in a chair and have him stand in front of you. And don't forget to maintain eye contact *at all times!*

APPENDIX C – EROTIC STORIES TO GET YOU GOING

Hopefully, by now you've gotten a feel for the naughty, nice, and fun way that I like to view sex. Here's a sneak peak into my vault of juicy stories that I write, when no one is watching.

FYI, some stories are cheesy and some politically incorrect, but I will not apologize for either, because they cater to various palates and honour all the cravings that've been shared with me, repeatedly.

Guy Meets Girl ...

I felt the gravel crunch beneath the wheels of my Dad's Chevy convertible, as I pulled into that final stretch, leading the way to a secluded beach. I'd always wanted to come there, with the top down, music pulsating. But I'd promised myself that when I did, I wouldn't be alone.

Tonight, I was definitely not alone. Her peachy skin matched the full moon; her dark hair, the velvety waves which moved almost as gracefully as her.

We kissed. ... We stroked. ... We walked barefoot in the sand. And then, just as I felt that strange mix of nervousness in my belly and firmness in my pants, she started to kiss me again ... deeper ... harder, this time. I thought I was going to explode from just that, since her body was pushing hard into mine, with nipples as firm as my cock.

Dare I open up her blouse, I wondered, even though I'd already groped her hundreds of times beneath it?

"Are you just going to stand there, staring, or are you going to take it off?" she asked impatiently.

With trembling hands, I struggled with her buttons, one at a time, until all that was left was a hint of a lacy bra, framing her ample cleave.

She ripped off my shirt next, not bothering to take her time with my buttons. It felt like my innocent Suzie had just turned into a vixen – a ravenously hungry animal of sorts.

More dancing followed more clothes getting ripped off, until we were both completely naked, able to feel every hot, wet sensation we'd caused within each other.

Finally, the dancing stopped, as she changed the music booming out of the Chevy to something more provocative. Her deep eyes stared into mine, as she mouthed, "The hood or the back seat? ... You pick."

Unplanned Threesome ...

My wife Tina and I were visiting with our long-lost friend, Cassandra, whom we hadn't seen since our good old collage days. Naturally both wine and gossip were flowing rather freely. And then, instead of heading out for dinner and a club, unfit drivers that we'd become, we decided to order in some Chinese, and catch the un-watched video which was still lingering from the night before.

Needless to say, all the sensual dancing and enticing masturbation scenes in Body Double started to loosen us up even more. The debauchery continued right through Chinese food and another bottle of wine. Alas, the movie stopped, but the hardness in my pants had just begun. Boldly, I swapped the video for a threesome video and left the room to prepare a chocolate fondue, while the girls huddled together on the couch, giggling.

When I returned, I found them naked, going at each other, mimicking the screen. Watching Cassandra's nipple in my wife's mouth was more than I could have ever hoped for; hearing their excited gasps and squeals, even more so. Next thing I know, Cassandra laid her head on my wife's belly, and began kissing her naked flesh. Slowly, she made her way down to her pussy. Tina allowed Cassandra a go at her pouty wet lips, while she squirmed every which way to make sure that her tongue was darting in and out of her, working hard against her throbbing clit. I decided to back off a bit, so as not to interrupt what was going on, and even tried to close the door ... almost the whole way, but not quite. But while I watched through the crack that I'd left open, the girls didn't seem to notice my presence, being too engrossed in each other.

It was now Tina's turn to give Cassandra pleasure. As the two swapped places, Cassy just opened up her legs as wide as she could, and pushed my wife's face into her juicy pussy. From the slurping sounds of my wife's tongue and Cassy's loud moans, I could tell that she was really aroused. I began stroking my cock, that was getting harder and harder within my boxers. And then, just as I was ready to explode, my wife invited me in, and offered me a blowjob, but not just within her mouth. She wanted to lick my balls while I penetrated Cassy's hot, wet pussy lips. On and on she went, her warm tongue indulging us both, until the three of us turned into one big mess of slick juices.

Cassandra went back the next day, after opening up a brand new door to us. ... Never saw her again after that, but that memory is as clear today as the night when it happened.

Professor/Student Encounter ...

I struggled through my class project, trying to tie up some loose ends before handing it in. But it was hopeless. I was stuck, due to the lateness of the hour and my fatigued brain, so it was time to call it a night. I'd just have to try again the next day, perhaps with the professor's help. And with that, I headed on upstairs to his office, hoping to slip a note under his door, requesting his assistance.

When I got there, the door was ajar, with the light on. Cleaning staff, I thought, and marched right on in, like I owned the place. To my surprise, it was him, burning the midnight oil, marking some papers. Our eyes met lustfully. Looking at the hunger in mine, he rose from his desk, closed the door, and pushed me up against the wall, his body firmly pressed into mine. I gasped excitedly, practically giving him an invitation to what we'd both imagined many a times before, yet never had the courage to pursue.

Sternly, he ordered me to lift up my hands above my head, and open up my legs ... wide. I obeyed, feeling myself get wet from excitement. He kissed me on the mouth ... hard ... as I just stood there. Then, he slipped his right hand inside my shorts to finger my pussy.

Next, his hands reached up beneath my T shirt, and started making exploratory circles on my belly, barely catching the bottom swells of my bare breasts. I hungered for him to go higher. He must have read my mind, because his circles grew bigger and bigger, making his hands reach up higher and higher. I gasped again, this time in response to him grabbing my nipples between his thumbs and forefingers, so he could squeeze them to my delight.

I could barely contain myself, when his hands finally slipped out, so he could carry me to his desk. With one arm balancing my exposed butt, and the other sliding everything off his desk, he cleared a space and lowered me onto it.

Next, he sat in his desk chair, reached for his scissors, and cut open my T shirt, from waist to cleave, spilling out my breasts at his mouth level. Slowly and deliberately, he indulged my erect nipples, one at a time, with his strong tongue, making me moan from ecstasy. And then, when I couldn't take it any longer, he yanked off my shorts and moved his attention from my upper cleave to my lower cleave. As he worked his magic on my pussy, I knew I was hooked ... I'd do anything for him ... go anywhere with him ... become his sex slave forever.

Older Woman, Younger Man ...

Steve planned to go trekking through the mountains in the Far East. Having read stories of exotic places, worldly pleasures, and scary scams, he decided to speak to Brenda, the queen of all exotic travel. No man or place worth discovering had ever escaped her. Yes, she was the one to talk to, though talking is all that Steve had planned on, her being 15-20 years his senior, not to mention experienced way beyond his 25 years.

As Steve walked into Brenda's place, it screamed of sex – incense, wine, and candles keeping pace with the pulsating music that her hips appeared to be swaying to, as she pranced about. Her silk robe, sans all else, clung to her svelte body here and there, thanks to a hint of perspiration, announcing that she was in heat. Anyone half her age would have been self conscious of it, but she wore it confidently, with great pride. Steve caught himself staring at her, and immediately shook his head to rid it of the lascivious thoughts that he was having, so he could get to the point of his visit – a quick conversation to prepare him for his trip. And not a moment too soon, since Brenda had caught him gazing.

"You know there's *no way* you and I are going to have sex, don't you?" was all she had to say, to get Steve going. What the hell did she mean by that, he wondered, telling him that it wasn't going to happen? If anything, it should've been the other way around, since he was the hot guy that every woman wanted. I'll fix her, he thought, with his mind going to all sorts of wild and crazy places.

Steve walked up to her confidently and kissed her aggressively, challenging her by pressing his hard groin against hers. She just looked at him with boredom, almost as if to say, is that the best you got – clearly she wasn't terribly impressed, since she was a sex goddess after all. Steve offered her a massage with her exotic oils, to ply her naked flesh within his strong hands. He started off with her back, then flipped her around to work her front. Her nipples got hard between his fingers, but he just ignored them and continued to move his hands down towards her pussy. Once there, he pulled her lips apart, to take a good look at them and beyond. Regardless of what she said, her juices spoke volumes to her arousal. Brenda pulled him atop herself and screwed him like he'd never been screwed before, taking command from beneath.

Once Steve came back to his senses, Brenda smiled and said, "I'd planned to do that the minute you walked in the door. And you fell for it, hook, line, and sinker."

Funny thing of it was, Steve didn't feel all that foolish, just having been devoured by the ultimate sex goddess.

Pick Up ...

Driving down a snaky, two-lane highway, just before sunset, I felt the heat rise between my legs, making my bikini bottom wet. Without as much as a second thought, I opened the ties on the sides of my thong, whipped it off, and then tossed it out the window, hitting a motorist passing by. Now I was left with a mere bikini top and a naked body, stuck to my leather upholstery, ready and waiting to be stared at, by anyone in a vehicle higher than my convertible.

The moment finally arrived, when a passerby saw my brazen invite to "look but not touch". Intrigued, he followed me down the highway, to my exit, all the way into town.

Hotter than ever, I needed to cool down with an ice-cream. But as I parked in the little lot, I realized that I'd have to do some fancy footwork to get my clothes out of the trunk, since I'd already donated my bikini bottom to a total stranger, through a carefree adventurous moment. Lucky for me, the rig that had followed me pulled up right beside mine, to help me out of my predicament.

He must've read my mind, because without as much as a hello, he asked, "What flavour?"

"You buying?" I responded. ... Following a nod from my bronzed, buff rescuer, I continued with, "Why don't you surprise me?" and watched him walk away, with the orange sunset behind him.

Anticipation was killing me. A few minutes stretched into hours – or so it felt – until he handed me a rather large, phallic looking cone, already dripping ice cream down its sides.

Don't know what got into me, but I flirtatiously blurted out, "Are you gonna get in or what?" while opening up the passenger side door for him.

It didn't take much convincing, for he immediately plunked himself down. I stared at his bulge, that seemed to get harder and harder while my ice cream turned softer and softer, under the pressure of the long strokes from my unrelenting tongue, licking salaciously to tease him. It was more than he could take.

And so, despite the fire within him, he mustered up enough courage to get out of the car, while he offered me his business card, for future rendezvous, should the interest grab me. But I wanted him right then and there, to grab my pussy and make me come.

How dare he! It was now my turn to chase *him* down. Maybe he planned it that way, but I just didn't care.

The Switch ...

Me and my lover were really getting into some sexy games – one of which was blindfolding each other and doing delish things without the other person knowing what was coming up next.

One time, in the spirit of the game, he tied my wrists and ankles to the bedposts with some silk scarves and then blindfolded me, so I could only receive, since we were both givers. Then, after teasing me for a while, alternating his touch between light as a feather and hard as a horny, rogue animal, he just left me there, squirming.

A while later, he returned, and barely traced my body with an ice-cube. Then, his hot tongue licked the goose bumps which stood erect all over my body, thanks to the anticipation of what could be coming up next. The whole deal was followed by the most amazing oral I'd ever received.

After a rapturous conclusion, I was kissed, soft and sensually, very different from usual. When my blindfold was removed, I found out why it felt so different – he had another woman in the room with us. To this day, I haven't a clue what came from him, what came from her. All I know is, embarrassed as I was back then, I wouldn't trade the moment for anything. Nor would I ever want to find out the actual details!

Card Game ...

Every Wednesday night, Joni's friends would come over to her house to play poker. Her hubby felt really put out, especially since he didn't particularly care for her friends. One day, he flat out told her, "I feel so left out when they come over. Wish you'd pay more attention to me instead of them."

Next time, just as the girls were arriving, and hubby was getting ready to lock himself up in the bedroom as usual, Joni blindfolded him, and said, "I have a surprise for you." He thought, great ... with all of them cackling downstairs, this should be good.

Joni lay her hubby on the bed, and giggled, "I'll be right back."

Sure enough, she returned, but with the girls. When hubby heard their voices, he tried to get up, but she said, "Not so fast" and hand-cuffed his wrists and ankles to the bedposts. Next, she blind-folded him using her silky panties.

Then, she ordered all of her girlfriends to get completely naked, and sit around him, since they were going to be playing poker on his body, after stripping him down completely. Poor guy tried to resist a bit – pretending to put up a fight – but then he gave in with, "What's the point? I'm out-numbered."

Once the poker game began, he could feel breasts brush across him, bracelets dangle across his cock, along with other stuff he couldn't guess, as the girls reached for cards. And then there was the occasional lick across one of his nipples, or the ridge across his balls. The girls sure gave him a hard time, making him absolutely crazy with all that teasing.

Then, just as he felt himself get harder than ever, they started to moan and breath heavily. Were they twiddling each other, or were they just teasing him, he never found out. But every Wednesday, he sure had a fun time trying to figure it out, not to mention all the fun he had with his wife, right after everybody left, every single time. Whoa!

Striptease ...

Gary used to love to go see exotic dancers before he married Rhonda. But since he'd given it up for her, one night, Rhonda decided to give him a taste of his favourite fantasy.

Right after dinner, Rhonda said that she was feeling a little tired, and was wondering if Gary wouldn't mind cleaning up on his own, and then joining her in bed. Gary thought, no problem, and did his stuff. As he went upstairs, he noticed that the bedroom was glowing with candles. What is she up to, he wondered?

Next thing you know, there's some raunchy music playing on the stereo and she tells him to sit down in the easy chair, right next to a fat wad of monopoly money. Soon, Rhonda came into the picture – and what a picture it was! She was hot, wearing a red coquette with cut out breasts, matching garter belt, stockings, G-String, six inch stilettos, and gold pasties with tassels. In case you're wondering, yes, she knew exactly how to twirl them. Gary's jaw dropped down, and he could barely mouth, "Come here, you."

She said, "Not so fast. ... What are you going to give me for a closer look?" Watching her dance, wiggling her hips this way and that, he pulled out a phoney 20. She laughed, moved back, and said, my rate is 50 bucks, just to come a bit closer ... and a 100 for every item of clothing you wanna buy off me ... to get a real good look.

Gary grabbed a fifty and motioned her to come closer. As he held it out to her, Rhonda brought her breasts right up to the phoney bill and squeezed them together to pull it out of his hand. Gary whipped out another hundred and asked if he could touch her thighs. She said, that'll cost you extra, while tugging on her garter straps. Gary started pulling out bills like crazy, anything to have her go for it.

Rhonda tugged on her G-String, and said, plant it right in here, big fella. No sooner did he do that, she grabbed his hand and started guiding it up and down her thigh, and finally let him barely slip it into her G-String.

Just as he tried to peel it off her, she pulled back a few steps and started dancing again, twirling her pasties, arching her back, moving her butt up and down the side of the armoire. Gary barely mouthed "How much for the G-String?" feeling like he couldn't hold off much longer. Rhonda hissed, "500", in the huskiest voice ever. He threw the entire wad of cash at her, pulled aside her G-String, and mounted her onto himself.

Spicing It Up ...

Joseph and his wife Ginny, married for quite a while, with a couple of kids to their name, had fallen into a ho hum sexual rut, where they just weren't getting hot enough for each other.

One day, as Joseph reached into his gym bag, he found a note that read: Meet me by the water cooler after closing. It's okay by Ginny ... it's her gift to you.

Joseph was totally blown away, and started to feel that strange mix of guilt and excitement, not knowing what was going to happen ... or for that matter, what he should do about it. He didn't want to hurt Ginny, but at the same time if this was truly something naughty from her, who was he to turn it down, and spend the rest of his life wondering? Torn as he was, he decided to go for it.

It was kinda dark. Joseph could barely make out the hot body that was leaning over the cooler, with long legs running up to a short little tennis skirt, and loads of reddish hair reaching down to it. Joseph remembered when Ginny's legs used to look like that in those tiny skirts. But the hair was definitely not anything like Ginny's short black, pixie cut.

Joseph knew that the hot chick could sense him coming, because she bent lower and started to wiggle her ass. Joseph dropped his bag and wrapped his arms around her, from behind. The redhead took his hands and shoved them beneath her top, so her braless breasts spilled right into them. Joseph felt himself get rock hard and started squeezing her breasts. ... Gosh they felt like Ginny's – there was that guilt again. But since Ginny had set up the whole darn thing, and there were no panties in the picture, Joseph pulled down his shorts and entered the wet and willing pussy from behind. As he started to come, he grabbed the long hair. It was a wig that pulled off, revealing Ginny's dark pixie cut. Ginny turned around and gave him the same smile she'd given him when they first had sex, many moons ago. Joseph realized that just because he'd thought it was the first time, it felt like it really was. "Just goes to show ya that we can have it back," is all he said, with Ginny grinning like a kid in a candy store.

"Of course I knew it was you all along" was the best save he could come up with after that.

Voyeurism ...

I focussed my telescope at her window yet again, ready to watch her nightly ritual. After all, she was the brazen queen of all things carnal, with her cadre of men, ready and waiting to satisfy an appetite that knew no satiety. Impatiently I waited, wondering who her Adonis would be this time, and how he'd try to put out her fire, if only momentarily. But tonight, she just danced by herself. Naked. Caressing her soft skin with an ice-cube. Who could blame her? The night was as hot as it was sticky ... or was it just her heat and stickiness which made the night feel that way?

The melting cube worked magical circles around her nipples, making them taut from a combination of part cold, part excitement. Next, it began following the long, stretchy drop it had created, right down to her lower lips – pouting for a touch. Wasn't long before the ice-cube disappeared, as did the fingers which held it.

I found my own fingers ripping off my dress, so they may mimic her lustful moves, uniting her with me, if only in spirit, right across a busy street, on a hot summer night. And then, as her aroused body fell to her satin duvet, so she may squirm and drool from her pussy lips writhing upon it, my adonis rescued me to my own bed, to take care of the heat within my groin.

But the voyeur in me transformed into an exhibitionist, and pushed him back to take a seat at the edge of the bed, while I brought myself to ecstasy, so he may watch but not touch ... taste, but only after I was done.

Summer Sex ...

It was a gorgeous summer day. My boss and I were dying to get out of the office, but still had tons of stuff to do. Staring out his corner office window, he looked at the shimmering lake longingly, like a kid who'd been grounded.

I asked if he wanted to call it quits for the day. He said, "Nah, we got way too much to do. ... But how about taking it outside – onto my sailboat?"

"Is that a trick question?" I asked, followed by, "You're the boss."

Next thing I know, we're lounging around on his boat, sipping pina coladas, him in his skimpy speedos, me in a string bikini he just happened to whip out from the galley – two sizes too small I might add.

And then, as we were trying to concentrate on work, my top whipped off; being too tight, the strings couldn't hold the weight of my massive tits. Embarrassed, I tried to cup them into my hands, while he only stared shamelessly, and said, "Please, let me do that for you." I took the boss's orders and let him take things into his own hands. Being no slouch, I followed suit, and got busy myself – funny how devil makes work for idle hands.

And then, as they say, one thing led to another, and hand action was replaced by some pretty wild mouth action. The unexpected, naughty little thrill was so incredible that it didn't take long for both of us to come. Hard.

Afterwards, we just lay there in the sun, buck naked, letting the breeze cool us off. And no, we never did get anything done, but neither one of us seemed to mind.

Tough Love ...

He was tied to a St. Andrew's on stage when she found him, his ass pink from all the whippings it had endured. One look and Domme-Unique knew that she had to sink her nails into that pink flesh. With a cold stare she glanced down at the two slaves she'd escorted in on leashes, their rhinestone collars glinting as they gracefully crawled on their fours, like Danes in heat. The male saw the lust in her eyes and winced with jealousy, the female jiggled her plump breasts to entice her, with what the tied specimen couldn't possibly offer. A swift slap, and Domme-Unique had her under her control, gushing out sweet juices from the excitement of being hit by her Mistress.

Domme-Unique's pencil-thin, high heels strutted up onto stage, and examined the gooseflesh which was now raw from excitement. Roughly, she undid the gag in his mouth, and shoved her lush breast into it – her long, distended nipples thrust deep into his panting mouth. "Eat this," she commanded, gagging him hard and strong. The slave's mouth felt good on her nipple. She wanted more. But his control over her desires disturbed her. It was time to control him instead, to resume the charge which rightfully belonged to Her. Domme-Unique began to whip his ass as he shivered and shook, helplessly tied at the wrists and ankles. The final strapping took command of his nipples, stinging an erogenous fire right into them. He was now rock hard.

With her expert hands, Domme-Unique began to stroke the shaft of his cock, up and down, while disallowing him the pleasure to burst, as desperately as he wanted it.

At long last, The Mistress finally allowed him a release, while her other two slaves brought each other pleasure, on Her command. ... And thus swept the rush across her face, from being totally in charge ... of everyone ... including her own pleasure.

On Becoming a Man ...

Rob had just finished his first year in college and couldn't wait to get home. His 23-year-old girlfriend was going to turn him into a man for his 19th birthday. All he could think of was, how her soft sumptuous breasts would feel in his mouth, while he impaled her between her soft sumptuous thighs. But as luck would have it, just 10 miles from home, his junk-box of a car broke down. Hard as he tried, he couldn't fix it.

The sun was beginning to set. Rob knew that the best he could do was to hitch a ride, and come back to his heap of a car the next day. His strong arms reached for his backpack and threw it onto the tarmac beside him. His thumb came out, and stood erect, waiting for someone to have mercy.

Wasn't long before a busload of collage cheerleaders screeched to a halt beside him. Was his luck about to change, Rob wondered? Judging by their enthusiasm to have a man come aboard, it would certainly seem so, outnumbered as he was.

Rob barely parked himself down, when they began "cheering him up". The way they were carrying on, teasing him like crazy, one would've thought they'd never seen a man before. But Rob wasn't complaining.

And then, just as he thought they wouldn't dare go any farther, a buxom blonde walked over and sat in his lap. Her ample tits supported a pair of sunglasses in their cleave. Rob tried to focus on the shades, lest he burst right there, right beneath her thighs where she could feel it. Watching him squirm, she said, "I'll just bet that you'd love to be where my sunglasses are, wouldn't you?" Before Rob even had a chance to respond, the blonde tossed aside her shades, grabbed him by his hair, and directed his face right into her cleave. Rob found his tongue licking the soft curves which formed the gully that he wanted to slip his hard cock into, imagining what it would feel like to pump her right there. ... But no, he couldn't let his mind go there, since he could feel himself getting ready to blow out his load ... not that it wouldn't feel good ... right across her voluptuous chest.

Quickly, Rob pulled back his head, and tried to look away. Being so preoccupied, he hadn't noticed that a redhead was standing right next to him, exposing her hot pussy to entice him. As he gazed at it, she pulled apart her lips, and tried to introduced herself, "My name is Cindy, but everybody calls me Cin for short." Rob just stared at her ... speechless. Cin went on to say, "Ever touched a pussy before?" Experienced as he wanted to sound, knowing full well that lying may have been a better idea, he blurted out a strong "No."

Aaah, a virgin ... just what the girls needed to kick into high gear. "Go on and touch it then," Cin ordered. Watching his hesitation, she gave him a bit of a push, "It wont bite."

Rob's fingers plunged into her pouty pussy lips, begging for his touch, and began trembling inside her. Cin bore down on them ... hard ... practically mounting them. ... Needless to say, that was all the rest of the girls needed, to begin touching and undressing him, on cue, enjoying the power they had over his virgin cock.

221

Rob saw smooth ones, bushy ones, nicely pruned ones, pierced ones; but the one which stuck out the most in his mind was, his first one – that glorious delicious one that belonged to Cin, because it started his unbelievable adventure.

As they say, no one ever forgets their first!

Chance Encounter ...

I admired him from afar, my groin wet from the anticipation of what it would be like to have him deep inside me ... impaling me ... the thrill of that first moment when tongues, lips, cock, cunt, tits, and all those heavenly juices slip into helpless, joyful confusion. He caught me staring. I shuddered, hoping he couldn't smell my arousal.

With the finesse of a man who'd done it a hundred times before, he walked over and barely brushed against the small of my back, making it ache from the smoldering desire growing just beneath. I wanted to drop to my knees, take his cock inside my mouth, and gently lick and tease him to the brink of release.

Alas, he must've read my mind – he took me aside, thrust me against a wall, and inhaled my scent. I felt his warm breath upon my neck; my body turned into gooseflesh, my nipples hardened into chocolate peaks begging to offer him a taste. I wanted him. Right then. Right there. His lips touched mine, his tongue slid softly into my mouth. My eyes drank from his as he slipped into my being, exciting me from the thrill of the unknown. Afraid that I was of what could happen – what I hoped would happen – I tried to walk away ... before I couldn't.

Moments later, the desire within me made me turn around, only to find him still standing there, leaning against the wall, stroking his hard cock. "Finger my pussy, you fool, to see how wet you've made me." I barked. Nonchalantly he fingered me, only to make my knees turn to rubber, my pussy drip from desire. One lick of his finger and he knew that I was ready for more. With a swift move of his right hand, he spanked my ass into submission. Without a moment of hesitation, I dropped to my knees and took his magnificent cock inside my mouth.

Tender licks led to passionate sucks, right down his shaft to his smooth balls, unencumbered by coarse hair. I could see my full red lips stretch this way and that, delicately teasing and torturing him with immeasurable pleasure. A moan escaped him as he oozed from his sex, allowing me a taste of his wonderful juices. Someone heard us ... we tried to hush each other, lest we get caught.

As the moment passed, he said, "See the trouble you almost got me into – for that I'll have to teach you a lesson." His strong arms lifted me onto a couch nearby, his fingers stretched out my pussy as he examined how pouty my lower lips had become, nicely framed within my garter belt, salivating at the mere thought of a kiss from his full mouth.

No sooner did I desire it, he delivered. His hot wet tongue began indulging my cunt – first the lips, then my hard clit, and finally my hot chasm. I found myself pulsating ... throbbing ... aching for him - what delicious torture!

It was now time for payback. Gently, I slipped one finger into my pussy, wet it, and then slipped it into his ass, knowing that it was sure to give him immense pleasure.

Like a trained magician, he began rocking back and forth, back and forth, demanding pleasure from my finger as if it were designed for no other purpose than just that. At that moment in time, indeed it was. I wanted to subject him to ultimate elation which knows no rhyme, no reason ... no control ... just the sheer experience of it.

Then, before he'd explode from ecstasy as I knew he would if I didn't stop, I lowered him onto the couch, laid him down, and straddled his face.

I faced him on my knees, shifting them farther and farther apart until the very core, the very heart of that hidden cleavage between my legs was split wide open and planted on his mouth.

Now we were engaged in a long, wet kiss, my lips of course being those other lips, smearing their saliva onto his.

"Taste it," I moaned, pressing down harder, circling faster, kissing deeper, forcing his hands to take command of my longing, hard nipples. No sooner did his hands tug and pinch them, throes of shudders squeezed slick juices out of my cunt, bathing his chin with ecstasy.

Nothing seemed more natural than me slipping my quivering pussy onto his rock-hard cock, my mouth taking command of his, our hands squeezing each others aroused nipples to the rhythm of our hips. The harder he fucked deep inside me, the harder his vice-like grip clenched onto my nipples, the deeper his bites sank into my flesh. Oh the pain ... the ecstasy! The ultimate control in knowing the power, which drives a sane man into a frenzy so strong that he's reduced to a mere animal right before your eyes. The thrill of creating a need which is unbound by limitations ... untamed by reason.

I had really only wanted to tease him, watch him squirm to make space for his cock as it got hard inside his slacks. Feel the thrill of controlling his groin when I knew he hated being controlled. At most, I would've reached over to feel the firmness I'd caused, stroke it like a pet, which had behaved on command ... and then walk away.

Little did I know that he'd have me dreaming ... desiring ... hungering ... longing insurmountably ... totally under his control!

Now it's time for you to create your own story, unbound by limitations, because this is *your* life after all – you go Girl!

About the Author

Dr. Rebecca Rosenblat is a Clinical Sexologist, Registered Psychotherapist, Certified Trauma & Addiction Counselor, Couples' Therapist, and Life Coach, critically acclaimed as one of Canada's leading influencers.

Rebecca has reached millions as a host of 7 TV shows & 2 radio shows; author of 9 books and hundreds of advice columns & articles; and as a workshop leader & keynote speaker at hundreds of events.

Beyond that, she's a clinical associate and private practitioner in Toronto, dedicated to helping people heal and grow. To learn more about Rebecca, you can Google her for her thousands of international contributions.

Manor House
www.manor-house-publishing.com
905-648-4797

www.ingramcontent.com/pod-product-compliance
Lightning Source LLC
Chambersburg PA
CBHW062136040426
42335CB00038B/1149